REFL
FOR **DAI**

REFLECTIONS
FOR **DAILY PRAYER**
NEXT BEFORE LENT TO **PENTECOST**

15 February – 22 May 2010

ANGELA TILBY
DAVID MOXON
JANE WILLIAMS
MICHAEL PERHAM
JEREMY WORTHEN
SARAH DYLAN BREUER
HELEN ORCHARD

CHURCH HOUSE
PUBLISHING

Church House Publishing
Church House
Great Smith Street
London SW1P 3AZ

ISBN 978 0 7151 4198 4

Published 2009 by Church House Publishing
Copyright © The Archbishops' Council 2009

The opinions expressed in this book are those of the
authors and do not necessarily reflect the official
policy of the General Synod or The Archbishops'
Council of the Church of England.

Designed and typeset by Hugh Hillyard-Parker
Printed by Halstan & Co. Ltd, Amersham, Bucks

Contents

About the authors

Angela Tilby is an Anglican priest in Cambridge and was previously Vice Principal of Westcott House, Cambridge. Prior to that, she was a senior producer at the BBC, where she made several acclaimed television programmes and series. She continues to combine parish ministry with her work as a freelance television producer, writer and broadcaster.

David Moxon is Bishop of Waikato, the Senior Bishop of the New Zealand Dioceses, and Archbishop and Primate of the Anglican Church in Aotearoa, New Zealand and Polynesia. He holds two Masters of Arts degrees: in Education with honours from Massey University, and in Theology from Oxford. He also has a Licenciate of Theology (Aotearoa) and a Diploma of Maori Studies from Waikato University.

Jane Williams lectures at St Paul's Theological Centre and is a visiting lecturer at King's College London. She taught previously at Trinity Theological College, Bristol.

Michael Perham has been Bishop of Gloucester since 2004, serving previously as a parish priest and in cathedrals. He was one of the architects of the Church of England's Common Worship and has written extensively about worship and spirituality.

Jeremy Worthen is the Principal of the South East Institute for Theological Education. He lives in Canterbury and is also an Honorary Theological Canon and Prebend of Chichester Cathedral. He has published on a variety of subjects, most recently on how Christian doctrine has been repeatedly shaped by encounters with Judaism.

Sarah Dylan Breuer is a public theologian and Anglican with a website, SarahLaughed.net, named by Beliefnet.com as among the best spiritual sites on the Internet. She is based in Boston, Massachusetts, but lists her occupation as 'have Bible, will travel'.

Helen Orchard is Chaplain and Fellow of Exeter College, Oxford. She was previously a curate in the Guildford Diocese and before ordination worked for the National Health Service. Her publications include works on John's Gospel and on spirituality and healthcare.

About *Reflections for Daily Prayer*

Based on the *Common Worship Lectionary* readings for Morning Prayer, these daily reflections are designed to refresh and inspire times of personal prayer. The aim is to provide rich, contemporary and engaging insights into Scripture.

Each page lists the lectionary readings for the day, with the main psalms for that day highlighted in **bold**. The Collect of the day – either the *Common Worship* collect or the shorter additional collect – is also included.

For those using this book in conjunction with a service of Morning Prayer, the following conventions apply: a psalm printed in parentheses is omitted if it has been used as the opening canticle at that office; a psalm marked with an asterisk may be shortened if desired.

A short reflection is provided on either the Old or New Testament reading. Popular writers, experienced ministers, biblical scholars and theologians contribute to this series. They all bring their own emphases, enthusiasms and approaches to biblical interpretation to bear.

Regular users of Morning Prayer and *Time to Pray* (from *Common Worship: Daily Prayer*) and anyone who follows the lectionary for their regular Bible reading will benefit from the rich variety of traditions represented in these stimulating and accessible pieces.

Monday 15 February

Psalm **44**
Genesis 37.1-11
Galatians 1

Galatians 1

Galatians is Paul's most passionate letter. We can almost sense the white-hot urgency with which he dictated it. Paul's Galatian converts are In danger of lapsing from his teaching because certain agitators are preaching a 'different gospel'. Galatians is a forceful defence of Christian freedom. It raises important issues about the sometimes competing claims of authority and personal experience in Christian life.

In this opening chapter, Paul lays out his credentials. He has received his mission not from human authorities but direct from God. The gospel he proclaimed to his Galatian converts was not an invention but a revelation. In support of this, he recounts his own experience of conversion from Judaism to faith in Jesus Christ. This biographical passage differs from the more distanced account in Acts (chapter 9). Paul's aim is to make clear that he has been set apart from birth for his mission. After his dramatic encounter with Christ, he does not consult with the church in Jerusalem, but goes away to Arabia. Yet, in spite of the singularity of his experience, Paul writes as one of God's family (v.2) and as one whose apostleship is recognized by other Christians.

Today's reading leads us to reflect on the paradox that, while the heart of the Christian gospel is deeply personal, we are never Christians in isolation. We are accountable to others, as they are to us.

COLLECT

Almighty Father,
whose Son was revealed in majesty
before he suffered death upon the cross:
give us grace to perceive his glory,
that we may be strengthened to suffer with him
and be changed into his likeness, from glory to glory;
who is alive and reigns with you,
in the unity of the Holy Spirit,
one God, now and for ever.

Psalm **48**, 52
Genesis 37.12-end
Galatians 2.1-10

Galatians 2.1-10

Paul's concern is the freedom of the gospel. He is convinced that Gentile converts are exempt from the Jewish law. The fact that the Jerusalem church recognized his mission as inspired by God shows that this argument was accepted. Further proof comes from the fact that the Gentile convert Titus was not compelled to undergo circumcision. The Galatians should trust their freedom! At this point, Paul's disappointment at what has been happening among his flock of Christians cannot be contained, and grammar and syntax abandon him. Those who are raising doubts on these matters are false believers and dangerous.

Paul's description of his meeting with the Jerusalem church differs significantly from that in Acts 15. But this does not mean it is inauthentic. Paul's chief concern is to persuade the Gentiles not to give up on the gospel. There were clearly real differences between Paul's version of the gospel and the gospel of the Jerusalem church. Yet both sides were able to acknowledge the grace given to the other. What Paul refused to recognize was the validity of the nagging doubts which his Galatian flock were prey to. Taking on the Jewish law was no answer to such doubts.

When the Church adopts an over-rigorous mentality, we need to be reminded of Paul's challenge and be confident in the freedom that Christ has won for us.

Holy God,
you know the disorder of our sinful lives:
set straight our crooked hearts,
and bend our wills to love your goodness
and your glory
in Jesus Christ our Lord.

COLLECT

3

Wednesday 17 February

Ash Wednesday

Psalm **38**
Daniel 9.3-6,17-19
1 Timothy 6.6-19

1 Timothy 6.6-19

The Ash Wednesday liturgy calls us to 'Remember that you are dust'. Our reading includes a sentence of scripture often used at funerals: 'We brought nothing into the world, so that we can take nothing out of it'. In this life, we are called to seek contentment rather than material gain. The virtues of righteousness, godliness, faith, love, endurance and so on encourage us to live balanced, sane and fruitful lives. God wants us to be human and humane, living wisely and within our limits, and he prepares us for the final revelation of Christ, when we shall see him as he is, in the splendour of unapproachable light. The Christian faith is a combination of mysticism and ethics, and it requires of us an active struggle. We must 'fight the good fight of the faith' (v.12) against our own less worthy inclinations – especially the inclination to greed.

Those of us who live in relatively prosperous circumstances need to challenge the materialism that is so casually endorsed by our culture. The accumulation of wealth is a response to anxiety, but all wealth is insecure and cannot bring us true peace.

Ash Wednesday is a good day to reflect on our dependencies and to imagine what it might mean for us personally to take hold of the life that really is life.

COLLECT

Almighty and everlasting God,
you hate nothing that you have made
and forgive the sins of all those who are penitent:
create and make in us new and contrite hearts
that we, worthily lamenting our sins
and acknowledging our wretchedness,
may receive from you, the God of all mercy,
perfect remission and forgiveness;
through Jesus Christ your Son our Lord,
who is alive and reigns with you,
in the unity of the Holy Spirit,
one God, now and for ever.

Psalms **77** *or* 56, **57** (63*)
Genesis 39
Galatians 2.11-end

Genesis 39

Today's reading introduces one of the great themes of the Hebrew Bible: the humiliation of God's people and their deliverance at God's hand. Read in a Christian context, the family saga of Jacob's sons looks forward to the gospel of forgiveness and redemption. The magic of the story is brought out in the much-loved musical adaption *Joseph and the Amazing Technicolor Dreamcoat*. Joseph, the favourite son of Jacob, has been sold into slavery in Egypt because of the jealousy of his brothers. Joseph has no control over his subsequent fate. He is sold and bought; he becomes a desirable conquest for his master's wife; he is thrown into prison in spite of his innocence. But he is still protected by God. His success as steward of Potiphar's house is attributed to God, and God remains with him when he is imprisoned following false allegations of attempted rape. Joseph retains integrity and so shows himself to be a true son of Israel.

The story provides us with an example of keeping integrity in times of adversity. There are periods in history and periods in our own lives when we have little control over the outer circumstances of our lives. This does not mean God has abandoned us. We can still bear witness to his greatness and power to save by living prayerful and truthful lives.

Holy God,
our lives are laid open before you:
rescue us from the chaos of sin
and through the death of your Son
bring us healing and make us whole
in Jesus Christ our Lord.

COLLECT

Friday 19 February

Genesis 40

There is something of the folk-tale in the story of Joseph, and this is borne out in today's passage. Joseph's fellow-prisoners are Pharaoh's chief cupbearer and his chief baker. We are not told what misdemeanours have led to their incarceration. The different outcomes that Joseph foresees for them contribute to the impression that justice in Pharaoh's Egypt is an arbitrary matter. Joseph, on the other hand, remains trustworthy. The captain of the guard puts him in charge. His gift of being able to interpret dreams is a sign of divine favour. Whatever injustices are perpetuated on the human scale, God remains the all-knowing and all-seeing who discloses the secret of the dreams to his chosen ones.

The human pathos of the story makes it memorable. The baker only dares to tell his dream when he sees that the interpretation of the cupbearer's dream is favourable. Yet the baker's hopes of release are dashed when Joseph unexpectedly foretells his execution. The cupbearer's head will be lifted up by restoration to office, the baker's by the ignominy of hanging. Joseph pleads with the fortunate cupbearer to remember him when he gets out of prison, but the chapter ends with Joseph left to languish, his plight forgotten. Are there people who have been kind to us and now need our help? It is too easy to forget the goodness of strangers.

COLLECT

Almighty and everlasting God,
you hate nothing that you have made
and forgive the sins of all those who are penitent:
create and make in us new and contrite hearts
that we, worthily lamenting our sins
and acknowledging our wretchedness,
may receive from you, the God of all mercy,
perfect remission and forgiveness;
through Jesus Christ your Son our Lord,
who is alive and reigns with you,
in the unity of the Holy Spirit,
one God, now and for ever.

Psalms **71** *or* **68**
Genesis 41.1-24
Galatians 3.15-22

Saturday 20 February

Genesis 41.1-24

Joseph languishes in prison for two years. But God has not forgotten him. Freedom comes when, once again, his special gifts as the favoured son of Israel are needed. Pharaoh's sinister dream of the fat cows and plump grain being consumed by starving cows and blighted grain has left his magicians and wise men baffled – or perhaps, more likely terrified. Their ignorance of the true God means that they cannot, or dare not, discern the meaning of the dream. Their confusion reminds the cupbearer of how his own fortunes were restored after a mysterious dream and triggers the recall of his one-time Hebrew cellmate. When the urgent call goes out to bring Joseph from prison, Joseph, ever-fastidious about appearances, ensures he is shaved and his clothes are fresh. He is ready to seize whatever opportunity is offered by his encounter with Pharaoh. But the real agent here is God. Joseph recognizes this by refusing to claim that his powers are his own. He points to God as the one who interprets dreams and whose answer will be ultimately favourable to Pharaoh.

Christians are called to discern the signs of the times, and this should never be merely in terms of condemnation. Even when the prospects for the societies we live in look bleak, we should point away from ourselves to God – the source of truth, wisdom and salvation.

Holy God,
our lives are laid open before you:
rescue us from the chaos of sin
and through the death of your Son
bring us healing and make us whole
in Jesus Christ our Lord.

COLLECT

Monday 22 February

Genesis 41.25-45

From Pharaoh's point of view, Joseph is no more than a foreign slave. But we know that he is a favoured son of Israel, who speaks for a God who has the fate of Pharaoh's kingdom in his hands. Joseph insists that Pharaoh's dreams are linked and that they disclose God's intentions towards the land of Egypt. The future cannot be altered. But Joseph does not leave the matter there. Seizing the opportunity to display God's wisdom as well as his warning, he suggests a plan of action for careful management in the good years, so that there is plenty of stored grain for the years of blight. Joseph comes up with a prudent plan for surviving future misfortune. It is obvious to Pharaoh and his counsellors that Joseph himself is the very man to take on the massive task of organizing the survival plan. So, Joseph becomes Pharaoh's viceroy invested with traditional symbols of office that can still be seen in ancient Egyptian tomb paintings and temple carvings.

Our faith may not bring us good fortune or the kind of stunning promotion that Joseph experienced. But it does give us hope in God's providence and access to wisdom in the management of our affairs, including our personal finances and resources. But there is responsibility here too – 'Much is required of those to whom much is given' (Luke 12.48).

COLLECT

Almighty God,
whose Son Jesus Christ fasted forty days in the wilderness,
and was tempted as we are, yet without sin:
give us grace to discipline ourselves in obedience to your Spirit;
and, as you know our weakness,
so may we know your power to save;
through Jesus Christ your Son our Lord,
who is alive and reigns with you,
in the unity of the Holy Spirit,
one God, now and for ever.

Psalms **44** *or* **73**
Genesis 41.46 – 42.5
Galatians 4.8-20

Genesis 41.46 – 42.5

Joseph has risen to a position of great responsibility. He sets about his task with characteristic thoroughness, ensuring that all surplus grain is gathered and securely stored. To crown these good years, Joseph is given a noble bride, the daughter of a royal priest. He names his first child Manasseh, signifying that God has made him forget not only his sufferings but also his homeland. But God has not forgotten Joseph's homeland, nor his father's love for him, nor the wrong that his brothers have done to him. There will be a reckoning, and the advent of the seven lean years provides the setting for that to take place. Jacob sends ten of his remaining sons to Egypt to petition for grain, keeping back Benjamin, the youngest son and closest brother to Joseph (35.24).

The reversal of Joseph's fortunes are now complete, and he is at the zenith of his power and prestige. How will he handle his greatness? And has he really forgotten his painful past? The story reminds us that we face particular choices to use or misuse the gifts that God has given us. Those of us who have others' well-being in our hands, whether we are parents, bus drivers or business executives, need to remember that we are entrusted with the lives of those whom God loves, those for whom Christ died.

Heavenly Father,
your Son battled with the powers of darkness,
and grew closer to you in the desert:
help us to use these days to grow in wisdom and prayer
that we may witness to your saving love
in Jesus Christ our Lord.

COLLECT

9

Wednesday 24 February

Psalms **6**, 17 or **77**
Genesis 42.6-17
Galatians 4.21 – 5.1

Genesis 42.6-17

The scene is set, and Joseph's childhood dreams of greatness (37.5-11) are fulfilled in circumstances deeply humiliating to his brothers. Never could they have imagined that the boy they sold to passing traders would be holding their futures in his hands. If they could not have foreseen this, then neither could Joseph. The interpreter of dreams now has the bitter-sweet experience of his own dreams being fulfilled as he remembers them, perhaps for the first time in many years. His harsh response is understandable, as the fear and humiliation he experienced as a vulnerable child when his brothers punished him for his arrogance now floods in on him. He cannot help but exact some degree of emotional revenge. He accuses them of spying and puts them all in custody.

Many of us live with family histories that cause us barely controllable feelings of shame and anger. Like Joseph, we may be able to live for years without dwelling on past horrors, but then memories are triggered and we can be overwhelmed. Yet God requires us to face up to the wrongs we have done and to the wrongs that have been done to us. Reconciliation is impossible unless there is truth on both sides. Without these, we are – like Joseph's brothers – prisoners of our past, and what we forget, we are condemned to repeat.

COLLECT

Almighty God,
whose Son Jesus Christ fasted forty days in the wilderness,
and was tempted as we are, yet without sin:
give us grace to discipline ourselves in obedience to your Spirit;
and, as you know our weakness,
so may we know your power to save;
through Jesus Christ your Son our Lord,
who is alive and reigns with you,
in the unity of the Holy Spirit,
one God, now and for ever.

Psalms **42**, 43 *or* **78.1-39***
Genesis 42.18-28
Galatians 5.2-15

Thursday 25 February

Genesis 42.18-28

Joseph leaves his brothers in prison for three days, by which time he has relented a little. He keeps a hostage and sends them to bring Benjamin with them. Joseph has another plan to test their honesty and display his generosity. The brothers reluctantly agree to the conditions. The command to fetch Benjamin has horribly reminded them of their mistreatment of Joseph so many years before. They now, as they see it, are paying the penalty for his enslavement – and possibly death – in the wilderness. Joseph, of course, understands every word and is overcome with emotion. He leaves the conversation and weeps. Then he makes the secret arrangements to have their money returned to them and to ensure that they have provisions for their journey. The discovery of the returned money in one of the sacks of fodder is the final moment of guilt: 'What is this that God has done to us?'

The story is heart-rendingly true to human experience. Family wrongs, even though long past, are never really forgotten. They wait to be discovered. When those who are wronged are willing, not to ignore the wrong, but to forgive, the perpetrator has to face up to what has been done. In the same way, God's forgiveness is often the spur that drives us to acknowledge sin. Where condemnation might simply harden our hearts, mercy brings us to repentance.

Heavenly Father,
your Son battled with the powers of darkness,
and grew closer to you in the desert:
help us to use these days to grow in wisdom and prayer
that we may witness to your saving love
in Jesus Christ our Lord.

COLLECT

Psalms **22** *or* **55**
Genesis 42.29-end
Galatians 5.16-end

Genesis 42.29-end

The old deceit of Joseph's brothers runs deep and includes the original lies about Joseph's fate that they told to their father, Jacob. Now they have to tell Jacob the humiliating story of their Egyptian adventure. To their dismay, more bags of money are discovered in their sacks. Jacob, in spite of Reuben's reassurances, refuses to go along with the requirement that Benjamin be taken to Egypt. Jacob is not without guilt in the family history. It was his indulgence of Joseph in dressing him in the 'coat of many colours' that provoked his brothers' jealousy in the first place. For now, he cannot face up to the threat of any further bereavement. He feels he has suffered too much and becomes incapable of action or decision.

It is often tempting in Christian discipleship to hold back just at the point where we need to make a change in our lives in response to a new challenge. We fear the exposure of commitment, because we are aware of deep vulnerabilities in ourselves. But vulnerabilities are sometimes exposed precisely because the moment has come for healing to take place at a deeper level than we thought possible. Redemption is waiting in the Joseph story, but it takes further disaster for it to be received. God always offers redemption, but we are not always willing to take the risk of making a response.

COLLECT

Almighty God,
whose Son Jesus Christ fasted forty days in the wilderness,
and was tempted as we are, yet without sin:
give us grace to discipline ourselves in obedience to your Spirit;
and, as you know our weakness,
so may we know your power to save;
through Jesus Christ your Son our Lord,
who is alive and reigns with you,
in the unity of the Holy Spirit,
one God, now and for ever.

Psalms 59, **63** *or* **76**, 79
Genesis 43.1-15
Galatians 6

Genesis 43.1-15

In the end, it is outer circumstances that force Jacob to change his mind. The Egyptian grain has run out. Starvation is imminent, threatening the future of God's promise. Jacob is called 'Israel', the name he was given by God (32.28, 35.10). This signifies his key role in the history of God's chosen people. He is not merely a pathetic old man in perpetual mourning for his sons. He *is* Israel, the one who has 'striven with God and with humans and has prevailed' (32.28). In the event, it is Judah who persuades him to let Benjamin go. Once he has made the decision, the old, scheming Jacob revives, planning little gifts for the mysterious Egyptian overlord in the hope of placating his wrath. He also shows that he is prepared even to risk a further bereavement for the sake of God's future.

The challenge to us is to continue to have faith in God's call to us. We are children of Israel through baptism, and our baptismal call is constantly renewed through the changes that life brings upon us. Circumstances alter, but God does not change. He knows us through and through, our strengths and weaknesses, and, if he asks more of us than we sometimes feel we can bear, he also supplies the grace and courage that we need to see his purpose through.

Heavenly Father,
your Son battled with the powers of darkness,
and grew closer to you in the desert:
help us to use these days to grow in wisdom and prayer
that we may witness to your saving love
in Jesus Christ our Lord.

COLLECT

Monday 1 March

Psalms 26, **32** *or* **80**, 82
Genesis 43.16-end
Hebrews 1

Genesis 43.16-end

If we are honest, perhaps all of us experience dysfunction in our family at some time or in some way – none of us lives in a totally 'functional' household or family all of the time. In Genesis 43, a father and his sons have to work out the consequences of deep dysfunction from the past and the present, offering a parable for family angst today. This family's issues are partly prompted and intensified by wider problems of the day – in this case, how to feed your family in the middle of a famine. As a consequence, Jacob's sons are sent on a journey, but Jacob knows from experience that there are huge risks. However, Jacob's faith in God is deeper than the underlying threats and dysfunctions of the story, some of which are even unknown to him. He lives in hope, even though he thinks he has lost a son on a similar journey before. Is this faith naive?

Although Jacob cannot see all ends, his faith begins to be vindicated by what transpires in today's reading. Joseph, unrecognized by his unfaithful brothers, offers them hospitality and grace, freely and undeservingly. Joseph's *shalom* has its origin in the mercy of God and, like a newly lit candle in the shadows, begins to dispel the darkness of dysfunction. Whatever dynamic is going on in your family, a faith like Jacob's can be a light in dark places, when all other lights flicker or die.

COLLECT

Almighty God,
you show to those who are in error the light of your truth,
that they may return to the way of righteousness:
grant to all those who are admitted
    into the fellowship of Christ's religion,
that they may reject those things
    that are contrary to their profession,
and follow all such things as are agreeable to the same;
through our Lord Jesus Christ,
who is alive and reigns with you,
in the unity of the Holy Spirit,
one God, now and for ever.

Psalms **50** *or* 87, **89.1-18**
Genesis 44.1-17
Hebrews 2.1-9

Genesis 44.1-17

Is Joseph a manipulative dissembler? Joseph appears to set up his brothers for theft and ends up making them face the moral dilemma that they faced years ago when they sold him into slavery for 'silver'. Should they abandon Benjamin, their father's favourite, and return home? Will they do to Benjamin what they did to Joseph? However, at its deepest level, the text is really saying that we all have an opportunity to grow morally and to learn from the past, and that life indeed presents us with many opportunities to test this. Joseph is seeking to get a reading on his brothers' moral centre, rather than wreaking revenge. Joseph is like a refiner's fire that does not cremate but provides the opportunity for hammering out a better result like beaten gold.

This is in fact what happens. Judah makes one of the finest speeches in the Old Testament, filled with moral responsibility and compassion. He even offers to sacrifice himself in place of Benjamin and thinks of his own father's grief if Benjamin were not to return to Jacob. The brothers must have thought that events were conspiring against them and a noose was tightening around their necks – and yet, this time, they retain their integrity.

Can we learn from them? Can we believe, even when we are outmanoeuvred, that our honesty and integrity will somehow be vindicated by God?

Almighty God,
by the prayer and discipline of Lent
may we enter into the mystery of Christ's sufferings,
and by following in his Way
come to share in his glory;
through Jesus Christ our Lord.

COLLECT

Wednesday 3 March

Psalms **35** *or* **119.105-128**
Genesis 44.18-end
Hebrews 2.10-end

Genesis 44.18-end

This speech of Judah has been described as a literary masterpiece, partly because it gathers up the whole drama so far in a powerful way, but also because it is a passionate and self-sacrificial appeal to a threatening authority by one brother on behalf of another. The speech is straight from the heart and lays out the claim for a family's love, grief and hope. The speech is also carefully designed to appeal to a menacing judgement. These words make it clear to Joseph that Judah and his brothers are so different from how they were when they sold the still unrecognized Joseph into slavery years before. A deep vein in this dramatic encounter is Judah's willingness to become a slave in place of Benjamin, a slave of the same Joseph whom he had made a slave all those years ago. Now he can sacrifice himself for his brother.

The searchlight of Joseph's inquiry can remind us that God's light is judgement as our soul is discerned for integrity and sincerity, but this light is also warm and life-giving. As this story unfolds, this is what happens for everyone involved: through Jacob's grief and hope, through Joseph's heart-searching and through Judah's self-giving. The light does not remove the pain or the complexity of the saga, but it does reveal the beginnings of a pathway through the shadows. So too for us.

COLLECT

Almighty God,
you show to those who are in error the light of your truth,
that they may return to the way of righteousness:
grant to all those who are admitted
    into the fellowship of Christ's religion,
that they may reject those things
    that are contrary to their profession,
and follow all such things as are agreeable to the same;
through our Lord Jesus Christ,
who is alive and reigns with you,
in the unity of the Holy Spirit,
one God, now and for ever.

Psalms **34** *or* 90, **92**
Genesis 45.1-15
Hebrews 3.1-6

Thursday 4 March

Genesis 45.1-15

We are witness to one of the most remarkable acts of reconciliation recorded in the Bible. This is a reconciliation that finally overcomes long-standing family distancing, falsehood, betrayal, envy and trickery. For the sake of reconciliation in this tragedy, Joseph steps outside the dignity, pride and security of his royal office and enters into the emotional complexity of his own family. Royal power will not heal the dysfunctions of his family, but empathy and vulnerability will. Joseph doesn't want guilt from his brothers – he wants the restoration of the brotherhood itself.

His inspiration and guide is God, who he believes has been working invisibly and unnoticed in everything that has happened in the family drama. This *shalom* of God can now be revealed. What God does is not dependent on the brothers' remorse. Joseph shares good news in terms of grace, partly because he himself has known grace in his own story. God has given abundant life *through* Joseph, rather than death *by* Joseph, and the brothers' own journey becomes the means for restoring this family to fullness of life again. God works within a situation, however sinful it has become, and constantly pours out the possibility of justice and grace. Even though the brothers have an evil goal, this is outmanoeuvred by the larger sway of God's providence and good purpose – bringing life rather than death. Such are the ways of God in the world.

> Almighty God,
> by the prayer and discipline of Lent
> may we enter into the mystery of Christ's sufferings,
> and by following in his Way
> come to share in his glory;
> through Jesus Christ our Lord.

COLLECT

Friday 5 March

Psalms 40, **41** *or* **88** (95)
Genesis 45.16-end
Hebrews 3.7-end

Genesis 45.16-end

This is a story of new beginnings. Joseph pours out a generous bounty and provision upon his brothers now that they are reconciled and restored in their relationship. Not only have a family's fortunes been replenished, but also the two nations of Egypt and Israel have a new bridge built between them; because of Joseph's family drama and the new life they have found, Pharaoh becomes generous. This is a bridge of solidarity, making a measure of justice and peace. As Tolkein once intimated, it is often the work of the many small hands – 'the seemingly unknown and weak' – that turn the wheels of the world, rather than 'the lords and governors', those who are thought to be in power and in charge.

For the family at home, Jacob, the grieving and surprised father, is given the grace to leave the past behind and work with the new potential that this gospel brings. Jacob is prepared to go to Egypt. Life and hope fill this family's life, and everyone begins again.

A family of brothers who were not able to speak in peace to one another (Genesis 37.4) are now talking freely, not only among themselves and with their father, but also with Joseph – and together they shape a new future. Enmity grows when the talking stops; hope arrives when the talking begins.

COLLECT

Almighty God,
you show to those who are in error the light of your truth,
that they may return to the way of righteousness:
grant to all those who are admitted
    into the fellowship of Christ's religion,
that they may reject those things
    that are contrary to their profession,
and follow all such things as are agreeable to the same;
through our Lord Jesus Christ,
who is alive and reigns with you,
in the unity of the Holy Spirit,
one God, now and for ever.

Psalms 3, **25** *or* 96, **97**, 100
Genesis 46.1-7,28-end
Hebrews 4.1-13

Genesis 46.1-7,28-end

Once again (cf. chapter 28), at a crucial moment, at a fork in the road, Jacob looks to his roots: to the faith that his family gave him, to 'the God of his father'. God responds to this faith in visions of the future. By a transforming vision, Jacob's fear is overcome; he is able to move forward to begin creating a new life for himself, his people and his descendants. Most poignantly of all, it seems that God makes this pilgrimage *with* them, rather than *above* them. God will enter into all the challenges, risks and opportunities of Egypt with them. The women and men who make this journey are going into an unknown future. This is the green edge of a new creation inspired by a faith in the God of their yesterdays, their present and their tomorrow. There is no past that God cannot redeem. There is no present that God cannot fill. There is no future that God cannot share with us.

We all 'contribute to the glory and tragedy of the divine life', as Peter Hodgson has said. God is intimately present in every choice we make and will follow us down whatever road we choose. When a negative choice is made, God does not abandon us but walks beside us looking for a better path. Their journey is God's journey. Your journey of faith is God's journey in faith with every choice you make and every path you choose.

Almighty God,
by the prayer and discipline of Lent
may we enter into the mystery of Christ's sufferings,
and by following in his Way
come to share in his glory;
through Jesus Christ our Lord.

COLLECT

19

Monday 8 March

Genesis 47.1-27

'To be a recipient of God's blessing does not in and of itself mean a trouble-free life.' This statement by Westerman reflecting on this passage means that Jacob's journey and his negotiations with Pharaoh show, yet again, that even a patriarch following a vision and a promise from God may have an unsettled life. When we hear God's call and are transformed by God's vision of a new creation, we must nevertheless be prepared for trials. Our calling does not mean immunity, but it does mean a profound sense of purpose and sometimes a sense of a peace that this world cannot give. Even in a life of faith overwhelmed by trials, hope can be perceived. It is despair that undoes us. Without a vision, we perish. Our own thoughts and feelings get tossed around by what happens to us – but, in quiet and contemplative moments, we may sense a deep pool of stillness that cleanses and refreshes. Worship in a strange place makes the place habitable. Your true home is wherever you are praying. You are the place where God lives. We sometimes have to make our physical homes and livelihoods in demanding and new circumstances one way or another. Although our story in Genesis 47 is very old, the faith, the hope and the creativity that it contains are ever new.

COLLECT

Almighty God,
whose most dear Son went not up to joy but first he
    suffered pain,
and entered not into glory before he was crucified:
mercifully grant that we, walking in the way of the cross,
may find it none other than the way of life and peace;
through Jesus Christ your Son our Lord,
who is alive and reigns with you,
in the unity of the Holy Spirit,
one God, now and for ever.

Psalms 6, **9** *or* **106*** (*or* 103)
Genesis 47.28 – 48.end
Hebrews 5.11 – 6.12

Genesis 47.28 – 48.end

'The Lord is my shepherd.' We sometimes sing these words from Psalm 23 at funerals and may associate them with death. In our story, however, they are associated with life and promise. God is a shepherd who guides, protects and provides food for the journey. Jacob knows that God is like this in life because he himself has lived the life of a shepherd and recognizes one when he sees one. A shepherd can be associated with the birth of lambs, as well as their oversight, care and sometimes rescue. This involvement in creation and redemption witnesses to God the Creator and Redeemer in all of life and in your life in particular, at this moment, as you are reading these words. The Lord is *your* shepherd.

W. H. Auden referred to God as 'always and everywhere present', so that our redemption is 'no longer a question of pursuit', but we can find God's very present peace in the very midst of our anxieties. Abraham and Isaac and Jacob all walked with God, their shepherd. We live in this blessing and are called to pass it on, which is what happens as Israel blesses Joseph's sons Ephraim and Manasseh. Each blessing is unique to us and our destiny. And we can bless even as we are dying.

Eternal God,
give us insight
to discern your will for us,
to give up what harms us,
and to seek the perfection we are promised
in Jesus Christ our Lord.

COLLECT

21

Wednesday 10 March

Genesis 49.1-32

The movie *Crash* was one of the first of its kind to depict a deep mix of motives, virtues and weaknesses within each character in the story. At one point, characters are heroic; at another point, they are cowardly. At one point, characters are honest; at another point, they lie. The good and the bad are found in each person.

This thoroughgoing reality in a story is present in our chapter today. The tribal groups that make up the people of God are a colourful mix of greatness and ordinariness, strength and weakness, goodness and evil – warts and all. It is only because God is known to be present and active within them, saving and blessing, that this warts-and-all picture of God's people is a picture illuminated by hope. This provides a kind of unity in the diversity, making tribal identity viable and possible for a new future.

The warp and weft of everything provides the texture of a tapestry woven by God. Muru Walters once said: 'Weave a cloak with different colours. Although the threads are different, they are threads of love and support.' This weaving image suggests that the very action of weaving integrates all varieties of strand – not only the strong, but also the weak and frayed – into a cohesive design. So it is with us.

Almighty God,
whose most dear Son went not up to joy but first he
    suffered pain,
and entered not into glory before he was crucified:
mercifully grant that we, walking in the way of the cross,
may find it none other than the way of life and peace;
through Jesus Christ your Son our Lord,
who is alive and reigns with you,
in the unity of the Holy Spirit,
one God, now and for ever.

Psalms **56**, 57 *or* 113, **115**
Genesis 49.33 – 50.end
Hebrews 7.1-10

Genesis 49.33 – 50.end

God always has the last word. God is universal purpose, in whom we live and move and have our being, and yet we are free – what a paradox. In this chapter, we see, in a world of free and sometimes destructive choices, the weaving-together of so many frayed strands and ends. God is a master weaver who can even integrate torn and frazzled material into the design of a greater tapestry. God does not cause the damage or the straying of ends, but God works with us nevertheless so that the overall pattern is not desecrated.

In this story, we see God achieve reconciliation through Joseph, working through the fear and guilt of his brothers beyond forgiveness to life and well-Joseph's sons Ephraim and Manasseh being. God is always behind the scene and invisible within the scene, yet is working at the green edge of the scene. God is majoring on goodness and mercy in an environment of freedom. God's plan 'is to bring the evil devised by the brothers to good effect' (Westerman). Sin and the outcomes of sin can never have the last word: God and goodness are a majority.

As John O'Donohue once said: 'On the day when the weight deadens on your shoulders and you stumble, may the clay dance to balance you.'

Eternal God,
give us insight
to discern your will for us,
to give up what harms us,
and to seek the perfection we are promised
in Jesus Christ our Lord.

COLLECT

23

Friday 12 March

Psalms **22** *or* **139**
Exodus 1.1-14
Hebrews 7.11-end

Exodus 1.1-14

Even in a world of many blessings, the possibility of oppression or disenfranchisement can occur. Tyranny may appear to arise and thrive – and even to be unconquerable. But, in the end, tyrants always fall, as the story of the Bible as a whole reveals. We need to think of this if we experience tyranny of any kind. That is why we can be challenged to turn the other cheek, that is why we may go the extra mile, that is why we may give our cloak as well as our shirt in an oppressive context, because we know in the end that God's justice is real, and evil is ultimately made up of hot air and shadows.

For Martin Luther King, 'Darkness cannot drive out darkness, only light can do that'. It has often been said that an eye for an eye by way of revenge means that the whole world goes blind, which is why Jesus told us to forgive our enemies while resisting evil. The transformation of an enemy comes about through good communication, patience and spiritual grace. As Martin Luther King also said: 'We never get rid of an enemy by meeting hate with hate; we get rid of an enemy by getting rid of enmity'. Can we live in this trust? What other hope has our world got?

COLLECT

Almighty God,
whose most dear Son went not up to joy but first he
    suffered pain,
and entered not into glory before he was crucified:
mercifully grant that we, walking in the way of the cross,
may find it none other than the way of life and peace;
through Jesus Christ your Son our Lord,
who is alive and reigns with you,
in the unity of the Holy Spirit,
one God, now and for ever.

Psalms **31** *or* 120, **121**, 122
Exodus 1.22 – 2.10
Hebrews 8

Exodus 1.22 – 2.10

These words depict one of the most famous scenes in all of history: the poignant, riveting drama of a vulnerable baby set adrift on a river by his mother in a desperate bid to try to save his life. The precariousness of the baby's destiny and very survival has captured the imagination of millions for over two and a half millennia.

The drama develops as three women, through a daring act of unexpected compassion, make visible the hidden providence of God and assure the baby's future. Pixley has noted that this Egyptian 'den of death' is still a place where God may find 'allies of life'. This is an astonishing liberation, which later makes possible the liberation of all Israel as Moses grows up to become their pathway to freedom out of the bondage of the Egyptians. The story has echoes of an 'ark' of life, ensuring the survival and liberation of Noah and his family together with their livestock. Somehow the deep taproots of Israel's story contain possibilities of justice and freedom no matter what. The people of Israel, as with the baby, have always been vulnerable themselves and, so often on the brink of being overcome by the waters of chaos, they still experience unexpected redemption from the hidden hand of an invisible God. There is always hope because there is always God – even when there is no divine sign, only a sense of faith in a God who mysteriously works within whatever happens.

Eternal God,
give us insight
to discern your will for us,
to give up what harms us,
and to seek the perfection we are promised
in Jesus Christ our Lord.

COLLECT

25

Psalms 70, **77** *or* 123, 124, 125, **126**
Exodus 2.11-22
Hebrews 9.1-14

Exodus 2.11-22

The people God chooses to be the heroes of his narrative are not obviously 'good', and the brilliant story-tellers of the Bible do not attempt hagiography. In a few brief paragraphs, Moses is depicted in all his complexity. He is a passionate man, with a strong sense of compassion for the underdog. Twice in today's reading, he rescues people from bullies: first the Hebrew being beaten by an Egyptian, and then Jethro's daughters being tormented by rude shepherds.

But he is also a rootless man. Although brought up by Pharaoh's daughter, he is not an Egyptian lordling. He cannot simply command the Egyptian he sees beating the Hebrew slave to stop, and he does not seem to expect his adoptive mother to shield him from the consequences of his actions. Yet he is clearly not accepted by his own people, either. When he tries to intervene in an internal squabble, they tell him exactly where to go. Expecting no protection or understanding from Egyptian or Hebrew, Moses runs away.

When the quarrelling Hebrews ask Moses who made him their ruler, they are setting a pattern for the whole of Moses' ministry. It is God who makes Moses their leader, not the people who choose him. In gratitude and in grumbling, the people will always make Moses feel just a bit of an outsider.

Merciful Lord,
absolve your people from their offences,
that through your bountiful goodness
we may all be delivered from the chains of those sins
which by our frailty we have committed;
grant this, heavenly Father,
for Jesus Christ's sake, our blessed Lord and Saviour,
who is alive and reigns with you,
in the unity of the Holy Spirit,
one God, now and for ever.

Psalms 54, **79** *or* **132**, 133
Exodus 2.23 – 3.20
Hebrews 9.15-end

Exodus 2.23 – 3.20

Moses, the rootless man, the alien, neither Egyptian nor Hebrew, living in a foreign land, is about to find his true identity – or, rather, to have it thrust upon him.

There is nothing in the story so far that suggests that Moses knows the God of Abraham and Isaac. He recognizes the numinous when he encounters it, but it terrifies him. And for God to introduce himself to Moses, who doesn't know his parents or his true family, as the God of his fathers, is perhaps not tactful.

What's more, God gets straight down to business, telling Moses how much he cares for the very people who have just told Moses to get lost when he tried to help them. So, it is very understandable that Moses should balk at God's simple assumption that he can be put to work for a God and a people he barely knows.

But there is a particular poignancy in the way Moses frames his hesitation: 'Who am I?' he asks. Nothing in his life so far has enabled him to answer that question to his own satisfaction. He genuinely does not know who he is. God's answer to him is, in effect, that identity is to be found in God alone, God the great 'I am', source, creator and foundation of all that is.

Merciful Lord,
you know our struggle to serve you:
when sin spoils our lives
and overshadows our hearts,
come to our aid
and turn us back to you again;
through Jesus Christ our Lord.

COLLECT

Psalms 63, **90** or 119.153-end
Exodus 4.1-23
Hebrews 10.1-18

Exodus 4.1-23

Moses really does not want the job that God has for him. His objections are very revealing: they all stem from Moses' odd, liminal position in relation to his people. In yesterday's reading, he had to remind God that he and Moses were not even on first-name terms yet. In today's chapter, that uncertainty has not gone away. Why would his people believe that he had met God? They had worshipped God all their lives, and knew the stories of God, handed down from one generation to another, yet God had not appeared to one of them. Why would he appear to Moses?

The proofs that God gives Moses are vivid and powerful. The people might cling to their religious identity in their slavery and misery, but they have forgotten that their God is mighty. Moses will need to remind them of that.

But first he has to believe it himself. He is still worrying about himself, his own inadequacies. He has still not grasped the character of the God of his fathers. In his head, he is already trying out speeches to convince his listeners, knowing they won't work.

So, God gives Moses what perhaps he needed more than anything else: family. He gives him his brother Aaron. Moses, the lonely man, now has a companion.

COLLECT

Merciful Lord,
absolve your people from their offences,
that through your bountiful goodness
we may all be delivered from the chains of those sins
which by our frailty we have committed;
grant this, heavenly Father,
for Jesus Christ's sake, our blessed Lord and Saviour,
who is alive and reigns with you,
in the unity of the Holy Spirit,
one God, now and for ever.

Psalms 53, **86** *or* **143**, 146
Exodus 4.27 – 6.1
Hebrews 10.19-25

Thursday 18 March

Exodus 4.27 – 6.1

Aaron doesn't need to be introduced to God, and he doesn't argue with the Lord's instructions, either to himself or to Moses. The story does not tell us anything about the previous relationship between these two, although it does imply that they knew each other reasonably well. How did Aaron survive the cull of Hebrew boy children that Pharaoh had imposed in Chapter 1 of Exodus? Is he, perhaps, older than Moses? Did they see much of each other while Moses was growing up on the edges of Pharaoh's courts? We just don't know.

What we do know is that Moses trusted Aaron. The minute God tells Moses that Aaron will be there to help him, Moses relaxes and accepts God's instructions. And now, with one kiss, Aaron takes his share of the burden of being God's chosen instrument.

This relationship is going to have to take a lot of strain. Together, they are going to have to confront not only Pharaoh but also their own timid and querulous people, and make them see the power of the Lord.

Neither Pharaoh nor the Hebrew slaves have any reason to believe that this God is to be feared. He is a God of slaves. Every day, they feel the might of Pharaoh, but their God has been only a quiet, nostalgic dream. All of that is about to change.

Merciful Lord,
you know our struggle to serve you:
when sin spoils our lives
and overshadows our hearts,
come to our aid
and turn us back to you again;
through Jesus Christ our Lord.

COLLECT

Friday 19 March

Joseph of Nazareth

Psalms 25, 147.1-12
Isaiah 11.1-10
Matthew 13.54-58

Isaiah 11.1-10

This shoot from the stock of Jesse unites all the hopes and dreams of Israel, drawing the world back to its origin and forward to its fulfilment. He arises from God's endlessly renewing and creative faithfulness, because he comes from David's family, but also because, in his rule, the Garden of Eden is reconstituted. He unites the roles of king and prophet, the institutional and the charismatic, the symbols of God's presence with his people, because he inherits the kingdom, but also because the spirit of the Lord rests upon him.

Because of him, the results of the Fall are undone: there is no more enmity between people and serpents, between one species and another. The 'knowledge' of God, which Adam and Eve tried to snatch, is now freely available for all, and fills the world with its pure and peaceful and liberating rule.

And what has this to do with Joseph? Is he there simply to provide the convenient link between David and Jesus, so that he functions as little more than a crossword clue? Or is something of God's own Fatherhood of his Son delegated to Joseph, glimpsed in Joseph, even, as he accepts God's rights over his life, and protects Jesus and Mary? Mary is not the only one whose yes to God brings Isaiah's vision to life. Joseph says yes, too.

COLLECT

God our Father,
who from the family of your servant David
raised up Joseph the carpenter
to be the guardian of your incarnate Son
and husband of the Blessed Virgin Mary:
give us grace to follow him
in faithful obedience to your commands;
through Jesus Christ your Son our Lord,
who is alive and reigns with you,
in the unity of the Holy Spirit,
one God, now and for ever.

Saturday 20 March

Exodus 7.8-end

For Pharaoh, this is still a contest about jurisdiction, and he is still confident that he will win. Why would be not be? He is the king of a wealthy and powerful state; he has been worshipped and served since birth, and, for as long as he or anyone else can remember, the Hebrews have been slaves. His divinity and power need no proof, whereas the god of the Hebrews has never shown any sign of life at all. Naturally, he is not going to let such a valuable workforce go after a few conjuring tricks.

Moses and Aaron, too, had grown up with Pharaoh's power as a simple given in their lives. They accept, almost humbly, Pharaoh's constant ridicule, his constant turning back on his word. They still feel themselves in his power, even as their trust in their God grows. Slowly, they learn that their God is not just the local deity of a group of hard-pressed slaves, but the Lord of all the Earth. He commands the great River Nile, the source of Egypt's trade, prosperity and life. At his command, it turns to blood – and, for the first time, it is the Egyptians grovelling in the dirt for the means of life, while their slaves begin to stand straighter.

But Pharaoh still believes that he is the greater god.

Merciful Lord,
absolve your people from their offences,
that through your bountiful goodness
we may all be delivered from the chains of those sins
which by our frailty we have committed;
grant this, heavenly Father,
for Jesus Christ's sake, our blessed Lord and Saviour,
who is alive and reigns with you,
in the unity of the Holy Spirit,
one God, now and for ever.

Monday 22 March

Exodus 8.1-19

It is interesting to note that, when the Lord sends Moses to demand freedom for his people from Pharaoh, he does not argue about human rights or about the injustice of the way Pharaoh is treating his slaves. Instead, he says: 'Let my people go, so that they may worship me'. This is the same Lord who will, later on in Exodus, tell his people that he is a 'jealous God'. His people cannot share their allegiance between him and Pharaoh.

Jesus makes exactly the same point in the Sermon on the Mount, warning people that, however much we would like to persuade ourselves otherwise, we cannot serve two masters. Only one will get the true service of our hearts; the other will get lip-service, at best. That is not enough for our jealous God.

Pharaoh is under no illusions: he knows that this is a contest for the heart and soul of the Hebrews. Pharaoh is a jealous god, too, as most worldly powers are. He doesn't mind the slave people having their own domestic religion, so long as it doesn't affect their true worship, their obedience to him. But he is not going to let them go and worship in freedom, because that would be an admission that their God's claim upon them was greater than his own.

COLLECT

Most merciful God,
who by the death and resurrection of your Son Jesus Christ
delivered and saved the world:
grant that by faith in him who suffered on the cross
we may triumph in the power of his victory;
through Jesus Christ your Son our Lord,
who is alive and reigns with you,
in the unity of the Holy Spirit,
one God, now and for ever.

Psalms **35**, 123 *or* **5**, 6 (8)
Exodus 8.20-end
Hebrews 11.32 – 12.2

Exodus 8.20-end

It is almost as though God and Pharaoh are playing a kind of deadly power game, with Moses and Aaron as pawns on one side, and the hapless court magicians as their equivalent on the other.

There is a set pattern to the game. The first nine plagues come in threes. For the first of each triplet, Moses goes to Pharaoh in the morning to deliver the challenge; the second plague is generally announced at Pharaoh's court, and the third comes without warning.

To begin with, the game seems pretty evenly matched. Pharaoh's magicians can manage the river of blood and the plague of frogs. But, towards the end of this first trio of calamities, when faced with the plague of gnats, they begin to panic. They know they are outclassed.

So, by the second triplet, which starts in today's reading with the plague of flies, Pharaoh has lost all his pawns: the magicians are no longer competing, whereas Moses and Aaron are still going strong. But Pharaoh is not yet ready to concede defeat, because if he did, he would have to admit that he is not God. So he struggles on, hardening his heart, refusing to notice that this is not a game of his invention, refusing to admit that, for all his famed power, he can only react to God's initiative and fail, over and over again.

Gracious Father,
you gave up your Son
out of love for the world:
lead us to ponder the mysteries of his passion,
that we may know eternal peace
through the shedding of our Saviour's blood,
Jesus Christ our Lord.

COLLECT

33

Wednesday 24 March

Psalms **55**, 124 *or* **119.1-32**
Exodus 9.1-12
Hebrews 12.3-13

Exodus 9.1-12

Pharaoh is one of the great villains of the Bible, but does he have any choice about his villainy when we are told that God hardens his heart?

This is exactly the conundrum that the comic book of Jonah faces. Jonah prophesies destruction on the people of Nineveh, but when they repent, God goes and calls off the catastrophe and forgives them, making Jonah into a false prophet.

At every stage of the narrative, God works with human choice, but people's choices get narrower and narrower the more they reject God. And that is exactly what we see in Pharaoh. Each time he chooses to deny the manifest power of God, his heart gets harder – and his choices diminish. He makes it more and more impossible for himself to admit defeat; more and more of his own self-image, his own pride, is bound up in this contest. If he had let the slaves go at once, he might even have gained a reputation for magnanimity, but now he can only lose the respect of all.

It is perfectly true that God hardens his heart. God doesn't have to do anything to bring this about – he simply has to exist, a constant reminder that Pharaoh's power is limited. Pharaoh could have chosen to acknowledge this obvious truth, but he didn't.

COLLECT

Most merciful God,
who by the death and resurrection of your Son Jesus Christ
delivered and saved the world:
grant that by faith in him who suffered on the cross
we may triumph in the power of his victory;
through Jesus Christ your Son our Lord,
who is alive and reigns with you,
in the unity of the Holy Spirit,
one God, now and for ever.

Psalms 111, 113
1 Samuel 2.1-10
Romans 5.12-end

Thursday 25 March

Annunciation of Our Lord to the Blessed Virgin Mary

1 Samuel 2.1-10

Hannah's song is a song of wondering praise for the God whose character she has just understood for the first time. Only verse 1 is about herself – all the rest is about God.

Although the song is anachronistic in this setting, since Israel has no king at this time, so verse 10 makes no sense, it is also appropriate. It is a pattern of grateful response, which we will see again in the Magnificat.

Hannah's story makes it clear how deeply she had been affected by her barrenness. Her husband's love could not make up for her sense of worthlessness, purposelessness. God's gift gives her not just victory over Peninnah, her fertile rival and tormentor; much more importantly, it gives her back herself.

But what is so striking is that Hannah immediately turns in love to God. What must God be like if he cares for one useless, childless woman? God's actions turn all the world's judgements on their head: it is not the rich and successful who have God's favour, but the poor and the hungry. For these people, to know God as our judge is to know hope and liberation. It is only the mighty, the rich, the oppressive and the wicked who need to fear God the Judge of all.

In Jesus, Hannah's God will be seen at work.

We beseech you, O Lord,
pour your grace into our hearts,
that as we have known the incarnation of your Son Jesus Christ
by the message of an angel,
so by his cross and passion
we may be brought to the glory of his resurrection;
through Jesus Christ your Son our Lord,
who is alive and reigns with you,
in the unity of the Holy Spirit,
one God, now and for ever.

COLLECT

35

Friday 26 March

Psalms **22**, 126 *or* 17, **19**
Exodus 10
Hebrews 13.1-16

Exodus 10

Now we are in the final trio of plagues. First there was the river of blood, the plague of frogs and the gnats; then there was the swarm of flies, the deadly disease that killed all the livestock, and the festering boils that infected all the human beings. And now, after the annihilating hail come the locusts and the darkness.

And yet Pharaoh is still trying to bargain. He is still expecting the rules of the marketplace to apply: Moses asks the impossible, Pharaoh offers less, gradually they come to a compromise. Egypt is facing an economic crisis on an unparalleled scale, so, under some pressure from his advisers, Pharaoh is prepared to make Moses an offer. He will let some of the people go. He expects Moses to negotiate, to thrash out exactly who will go and who will stay. Both will be able to go back to their people and announce a victory.

But Moses is not negotiating. Pharaoh is still thinking of the Hebrews as his slaves, people over whom he has absolute right of life and death. He simply cannot get it into his head that they are God's people, not his.

It is Pharaoh who brings negotiations to an end, saying that he never wants to see Moses again. For once, he is going to get his way.

COLLECT

Most merciful God,
who by the death and resurrection of your Son Jesus Christ
delivered and saved the world:
grant that by faith in him who suffered on the cross
we may triumph in the power of his victory;
through Jesus Christ your Son our Lord,
who is alive and reigns with you,
in the unity of the Holy Spirit,
one God, now and for ever.

Exodus 11

How Moses has changed! Throughout Egypt, and even at court, Moses is known and respected. He is now facing Pharaoh as an equal, not afraid to show his anger to this great ruler, who would never have been spoken to like this before. Pharaoh's officials are no longer trying to hide the fact that they fear Moses more than they fear Pharaoh.

Moses' confidence has grown so that he no longer automatically speaks through Aaron. Now he is able to deliver God's messages himself.

Moses' people, the Hebrew slaves, are benefiting, too, from the respect Moses has won. They have been very visibly protected from the dreadful effects of the torments that Pharaoh has failed to avert for his own people, and now their Egyptian neighbours suddenly want to give them expensive presents and curry favour with these people whom, just a few days before, they would have treated like dogs.

But Pharaoh's bargaining days are over. He no longer has the power to make choices. God no longer says: 'Let my people go, or else …' Moses announces this last, terrible curse as something that is bound to happen. This one stands alone, not part of the repeating pattern of three trios that has characterized the other plagues. Pharaoh is about to lose something that all his wealth, power and status cannot shield.

Gracious Father,
you gave up your Son
out of love for the world:
lead us to ponder the mysteries of his passion,
that we may know eternal peace
through the shedding of our Saviour's blood,
Jesus Christ our Lord.

COLLECT

37

Monday 29 March

Monday of Holy Week

Lamentations 1.1-12a

Our eyes have been turned on to the city of Jerusalem since Jesus rode into it yesterday, on Palm Sunday, in that triumphal procession that also felt like a beginning of the walk to the cross. But the writer of Lamentations takes us back far into the city's history in his lament over its desolation. He is writing, almost certainly, of its fall to the Babylonians 600 years before. The city he describes is a place of affliction, shortage and servitude, deserted by people driven into exile. Even the temple and its sanctuary have been violated.

Yet the Jerusalem that Jesus entered was not a ruin. It had been rebuilt, temple and all. The sense of desolation has shifted from the city to the one single person, who is taking upon himself all the hurt, treachery and mockery, and beginning the journey that will take him outside the city to the place where he will suffer for the multitude of the transgressions, not just of the people of the city, but of the whole human race.

It is as if Jesus, rather than the city, cries out: 'Is it nothing to you, all you who pass by? Look and see if there is any sorrow like my sorrow' (v.12). And that is his invitation in Holy Week – look, *really look*, and see his sorrows.

COLLECT

Almighty and everlasting God,
who in your tender love towards the human race
    sent your Son our Saviour Jesus Christ
to take upon him our flesh
and to suffer death upon the cross:
grant that we may follow the example of his patience and
    humility,
and also be made partakers of his resurrection;
through Jesus Christ your Son our Lord,
who is alive and reigns with you,
in the unity of the Holy Spirit,
one God, now and for ever.

Psalm 27
Lamentations 3.1-18
Luke 22.[24-38] 39-53

Tuesday 30 March

Tuesday of Holy Week

Lamentations 3.1-18

The Christian explores the death of Jesus through the lens of the resurrection. We cannot pretend we do not know what will happen at Easter. Nevertheless, we want to get inside the mind of Christ in Holy Week, so as to share his experience, as much as we can, not just out of love for him, but also so that we may learn how to handle deep darkness and desolation in our own lives.

In reading the words of this passage, and stopping where the lectionary does, we apply the words of Lamentations to a Jesus who is losing the sense of God's love and protection. He is being made to sit in darkness. His way is blocked with hewn stones. He says: 'Gone is my glory' (v.18). Human experience recognizes that in every life there are times like that.

But the writer does not stop at verse 18. He goes on to say: 'The steadfast love of the Lord never ceases, his mercies never come to an end; they are new every morning; great is your faithfulness' (vv.22-23). And, even in Holy Week, we engage with a God who drives out darkness with light, who speaks of the cross in terms of glory and who, far from blocking the way with hewn stones, will roll back the stone on Easter Day. Yes, we explore the death through the lens of the resurrection.

True and humble king,
hailed by the crowd as Messiah:
grant us the faith to know you and love you,
that we may be found beside you
on the way of the cross,
which is the path of glory.

COLLECT

Wednesday 31 March

Wednesday of Holy Week

Psalm 102 [*or* 102.1-18]
Jeremiah 11.18-20
Luke 22.54-end

Jeremiah 11.18-20

Jeremiah portrays himself as a gentle lamb led to the slaughter and, seeing it on this day when Judas plots with the authorities to have Jesus led away, the picture fits Jesus also. It is a different image from the one that Jesus himself has used in his teaching. There, he is the shepherd, the good shepherd who lays down his life for his sheep.

Both images are helpful: the shepherd because it reveals a Jesus knowingly and actively embracing his vocation, the lamb because it reveals a willingness to be led, passively allowing others to do to him what they will. And there is a sense that, in his passion, Jesus does move from activity to passivity. He is 'handed over' – and not just by Judas.

Scripture and liturgy keep bringing the two images before us, so that we can let them interact in our reflections. At every Eucharist, we pray: 'Lamb of God, you take away the sin of the world'. Through the weeks of Easter, we will hear in the blessing of the 'God of peace who brought again from the dead our Lord Jesus, that great Shepherd of the sheep, through the blood of the everlasting covenant'. The Book of Revelation gives glory 'to the one seated on the throne and to the Lamb' (5.13). Shepherd and Lamb – Christ is both for us as he goes to his death.

COLLECT

Almighty and everlasting God,
who in your tender love towards the human race
    sent your Son our Saviour Jesus Christ
to take upon him our flesh
and to suffer death upon the cross:
grant that we may follow the example of his patience
    and humility,
and also be made partakers of his resurrection;
through Jesus Christ your Son our Lord,
who is alive and reigns with you,
in the unity of the Holy Spirit,
one God, now and for ever.

Psalms 42, 43
Leviticus 16.2-24
Luke 23.1-25

Maundy Thursday

Leviticus 16.2-24

There are just enough words in this passage to make us feel we are on the familiar ground of Christian worship – vestments, offerings, incense, sanctuary, altar. But a closer look reveals a ritual entirely different from the one that Christians celebrate on Maundy Thursday evening. For, in its description of the ritual of atonement, Leviticus is describing the slaughter of bulls and the driving of a 'scapegoat' into the wilderness. This is the old covenant, one that Jesus supersedes, one that Scripture says can never take sins away, however much blood is shed.

Jesus gathers tonight with his friends in the upper room, no animal in sight, just bread and wine upon the table. Taking them into his hands, he speaks of his body and his blood. If this is the beginning of a ritual of atonement, it is very different, an utterly new covenant. The supper over, there is no goat driven into the wilderness – but Jesus himself willingly goes out into the night, himself a kind of scapegoat, and something of his wilderness experience comes back to him in the garden. Tomorrow, the cross may seem to be a kind of altar on which a sacrifice is made, but it will not be the blood of animals but the pure offering of himself by the great high priest, Jesus Christ, not clad in holy vestments but hanging naked for the sin of the world.

True and humble king,
hailed by the crowd as Messiah:
grant us the faith to know you and love you,
that we may be found beside you
on the way of the cross,
which is the path of glory.

COLLECT

Friday 2 April

Good Friday

Psalm 69
Genesis 22.1-18
John 19.38-end *or* Hebrews 10.1-10

Genesis 22.1-18

It is a dreadful story, Abraham setting out to sacrifice his beloved son. Inevitably, we ask whether this really was God testing Abraham. Was Abraham simply misunderstanding a God who would never make such an awful demand? The Christian tradition might have left it among the other obscure stories that are hidden in the Scriptures but not given much exposure.

Instead, the story is given prominence, read on the morning when Jesus hangs upon the cross, himself a sacrifice, an offering for the sin of the world. It could once again look like the work of an unacceptable God, demanding something dreadful of a beloved son. And, as such, we might want to turn away from it and, at the same time, be thankful that our understanding of God has moved on. The God in whom we believe doesn't need to punish the innocent in order to appease his anger.

But, as we gaze at the cross, we are looking not at one punished by a wrathful God, but at God himself. God did not require some other to demonstrate his love and compassion. In the mystery of the Trinity, this is God incarnate shouldering all this himself. The God of love ascends the cross and from it looks out in compassion on the world that he alone redeems.

COLLECT

Almighty Father,
look with mercy on this your family
for which our Lord Jesus Christ was content to be betrayed
    and given up into the hands of sinners
    and to suffer death upon the cross;
who is alive and glorified with you and the Holy Spirit,
one God, now and for ever.

Psalm 142
Hosea 6.1-6
John 2.18-22

Hosea 6.1-6

It is a day of waiting, a kind of no man's land. Nothing happens on Easter Eve. Jesus is dead and buried, and that is that. There's some looking back, of course, to a horrible day. Hosea can write of a moment when God punished his people, 'hewn by the prophets', and killed them by the words of his mouth (v.5). Very differently from that, on Good Friday, the punishment was by the people, and they punished not just a prophet but the Son, killing him who was the Word of God himself.

There is some looking forward, too. 'After two days he will revive us; on the third day he will raise us up' (v.2). Applied to Jesus, it becomes a trusting hope in the resurrection that Easter will bring, when Christ's appearing will be as sure as the dawn.

But, meanwhile, there is the waiting. R. S. Thomas, in his poem *Kneeling*, says simply 'the meaning is in the waiting' – and that is true to Christian experience. Jesus waits patiently for his salvation to come, for the Father to draw him by his love back into life. Often, we can let go of a painful past and can even see some light at the end of a dark tunnel. But there has to be the patient waiting until the time is right.

Grant, Lord,
that we who are baptized into the death
of your Son our Saviour Jesus Christ
may continually put to death our evil desires
and be buried with him;
and that through the grave and gate of death
we may pass to our joyful resurrection;
through his merits,
who died and was buried and rose again for us,
your Son Jesus Christ our Lord.

COLLECT

43

Monday 5 April

Monday of Easter Week

1 Corinthians 15.1-11

Through the Easter season, Christians will explore the resurrection stories, one by one, rejoicing as each one proclaims that Christ is risen. But, as if we cannot wait to unpack them by one, these opening verses of 1 Corinthians 15 are given to us on only the second day of Easter, with Paul pouring out a whole list of resurrection appearances – interestingly, most of them different from the ones the Gospels recount.

Equally interesting is that Paul apparently has no interest in empty-tomb stories. For him, what matters are resurrection appearances, people encountering the Risen Lord. His list of these encounters reaches a kind of climax with his 'Last of all, as to someone untimely born, he appeared also to me'. That appearance, the gracious confrontation on the Damascus Road that we call Paul's conversion, was long after the ascension and the giving of the Spirit at Pentecost, yet Paul experiences it as a resurrection appearance.

That encourages us to see our own moments of encounter with Jesus Christ as appearances of the Risen Lord. And, though we will value the story of the empty tomb and the appearances long ago to Mary Magdalene, Thomas and the others, we shall know that the evidence of the resurrection is that we too have met the Risen Lord. He is risen indeed. Alleluia!

COLLECT

Lord of all life and power,
who through the mighty resurrection of your Son
overcame the old order of sin and death
to make all things new in him:
grant that we, being dead to sin
and alive to you in Jesus Christ,
may reign with him in glory;
to whom with you and the Holy Spirit
be praise and honour, glory and might,
now and in all eternity.

Psalms 112, 147.1-12
Exodus 12.14-36
1 Corinthians 15.12-19

Tuesday 6 April

Tuesday of Easter Week

1 Corinthians 15.12-19

Doubts about the resurrection are nothing new. Paul is dealing with doubt both about the resurrection of the dead in general and the resurrection of Jesus in particular. At the first Easter, Jesus himself had addressed the doubts of Thomas, inviting him to reach out his hand and put it in Jesus' side and to abandon doubt in favour of belief. It elicited from Thomas that profound expression of faith, 'My Lord and my God', which claimed more for Jesus than any had done before.

For Paul, belief in the resurrection is absolutely central. He holds as equally important both that the dead in general are raised and that Jesus was raised. In his teaching, for all that the resurrection is for the present, changing lives, as it had Thomas's life and Paul's own life, it is also for the future – 'If for this life only we have hoped in Christ, we are of all people most to be pitied' (v.19).

In a week with cascades of alleluias as the Church celebrates a Risen Lord present in its midst in the here and now, Paul wants us also to believe in relation to the future and to rejoice. That Christ is risen is good news – not only for us now, but also for those who have died – and will also be good news for us when our life on earth comes to its end. More alleluias!

God of glory,
by the raising of your Son
you have broken the chains of death and hell:
fill your Church with faith and hope;
for a new day has dawned
and the way to life stands open
in our Saviour Jesus Christ.

COLLECT

45

Wednesday 7 April

Wednesday of Easter Week

Psalms **113**, 147.13-end
Exodus 12.37-end
1 Corinthians 15.20-28

1 Corinthians 15.20-28

The First Prayer Book of Edward VI in 1549 ordered at Easter the saying or singing of an Easter anthem, bringing together verses from Romans and 1 Corinthians. They have been part of Anglican devotion ever since. They include these verses from 1 Corinthians 15 (Authorized Version): 'For since by man came death, by man came also the resurrection of the dead. For as in Adam all die, even so in Christ shall all be made alive.'

We are given an image of Jesus as the new Adam. The first Adam, who represents the old humanity, brings sin and death into the world through his disobedience – sin and death represented by a tree from which forbidden fruit is taken. The second Adam, Jesus, the one who inaugurates a new humanity, himself the fruit of another tree, the cross, conquers sin and death and restores life, opening up a way to a new and eternal life.

Bishop John V. Taylor used often to say that 'God does not care very much whether you are religious, but he does care that you should be alive'. Jesus himself spoke of coming to bring life in all its fullness. Paul is telling us that this aliveness is a fruit of the resurrection. The deadness of Adam, of the old humanity, has gone. In Christ, all is made alive. The Prayer Book of 1549 wisely added to the text three alleluias!

COLLECT

Lord of all life and power,
who through the mighty resurrection of your Son
overcame the old order of sin and death
to make all things new in him:
grant that we, being dead to sin
and alive to you in Jesus Christ,
may reign with him in glory;
to whom with you and the Holy Spirit
be praise and honour, glory and might,
now and in all eternity.

Psalms **114**, 148
Exodus 13.1-16
1 Corinthians 15.29-34

Thursday of Easter Week

1 Corinthians 15.29-34

Paul is piling on the arguments for belief in resurrection life for the dead. There was clearly a practice at Corinth of receiving baptism on behalf of the dead. How widespread it was we do not know, and clearly it was not a practice that took hold. But Paul's point, in any case, is to say something not about baptism but about the existence of people who have died and who need to be brought into the fullness of resurrection life. Then he moves on to talk about his motive for fighting 'with wild beasts at Ephesus'. The commentators are united in believing that this is a metaphor for challenging experiences that Paul faced there, rather than a factual account of a trial of strength in the arena. But, again, Paul's motive for writing is to assert that there is a hope for eternal life, rather than simply a human hope for this life, that drives him on.

The message is clear. Whatever the Christian does, even if it concerns the things of today and seems to relate to life on this planet in the present, needs to have an eye to the future, a vision of heaven and a certainty that there lies ahead of us a life beyond this one. It is the death and resurrection of Jesus that open the door to this wonderful possibility. That is a truth that calls forth another Easter alleluia!

God of glory,
by the raising of your Son
you have broken the chains of death and hell:
fill your Church with faith and hope;
for a new day has dawned
and the way to life stands open
in our Saviour Jesus Christ.

COLLECT

47

Friday 9 April

Friday of Easter Week

Psalms **115**, 149
Exodus 13.17 – 14.14
1 Corinthians 15.35-50

1 Corinthians 15.35-50

The Jesus of the resurrection was recognizably the same Jesus who faced death on a cross, but not always immediately so and certainly not exactly so. Mary in the garden thought he was the gardener. The two who walked to Emmaus had a long conversation in which Jesus' identity was hidden. Only when he broke the bread at the supper table did they recognize him. His resurrection body could come and go and slip through locked doors. The bodily Jesus on Easter Day was recognizable but different. He had been raised by the Father in glory and in power.

Paul explores here the degree of continuity and discontinuity between our earthly physical body and the heavenly spiritual body with which we will one day be clothed. The one is related to the other, for he shows that there is a biological continuity in the process from death to life and that the life into which the seed is transformed is a richer and fuller one.

His concern is with our life after death. In Easter Week, our own concern may be more focused on the risen Lord and the continuity and discontinuity of his body. As the Gospels recount it, here was a more glorious body, vibrant with God-given new life, but, crucially, still bearing the scars of his passion. For all eternity and for all humanity, he bears the scars. Alleluia!

COLLECT

Lord of all life and power,
who through the mighty resurrection of your Son
overcame the old order of sin and death
to make all things new in him:
grant that we, being dead to sin
and alive to you in Jesus Christ,
may reign with him in glory;
to whom with you and the Holy Spirit
be praise and honour, glory and might,
now and in all eternity.

Psalms **116**, 150
Exodus 14.15-end
1 Corinthians 15.51-end

Saturday 10 April

Saturday of Easter Week

1 Corinthians 15.51-end

As Easter Week comes to its end, Paul reaches the climax of his long outpouring about the resurrection. It has begun with the unique resurrection of one man, Jesus Christ. 'Christ died for our sins,' Paul has said, 'was buried and was raised on the third day in accordance with the scriptures.' Paul has given witness to his own experience of the Risen Lord and that of other individuals, but then he takes off into an impassioned exploration of how this pattern of resurrection is for all, at least for all Christian believers.

'Death has been swallowed up in victory', he claims, quoting Isaiah 25.8, which pictures the life to come as a joyful feast, and he takes two pessimistic questions from Hosea 13.14 that reflect God's judgement on Israel and turns them into rhetorical questions of hope and faith: 'Where, O death, is your victory? Where, O death, is your sting?'

The victory is Christ's – and, confident in this faith, his readers are to be steadfast and immovable, and engaged in the Lord's work. In other words, the Easter good news is not just something to celebrate, but something to live out in lives of faith and in sharing God's mission. One day, God will act decisively to bring the present order to an end, and we shall all be changed. Meanwhile, in the light of the resurrection, there is work to be done. Alleluia!

God of glory,
by the raising of your Son
you have broken the chains of death and hell:
fill your Church with faith and hope;
for a new day has dawned
and the way to life stands open
in our Saviour Jesus Christ.

COLLECT

49

Monday 12 April

Exodus 15.1-21

'How can I keep from singing?' It's the refrain of a Quaker hymn, and in this passage joy overflows into song. What an amazing thing God has done in delivering his people! How can Moses and Miriam and everyone else keep from singing?

But this song does more than express emotion. It celebrates how God has acted at the Red Sea by making it one act within a whole drama. The overcoming of watery chaos reminds us of how it all began with creation (see Isaiah 51.9-10). For those who have just escaped from Egypt, the other side of the Jordan and the home to be established there can already be glimpsed and affirmed: Israel flourishing in God's abode, his holy place (v.17). Egypt and Pharaoh are not named after the opening verses, as the song finds in this unique event the pattern of God's deliverance of us from danger and death time and time again. It is a pattern illuminated for ever by the encounter of Easter morning.

In other words, what we are reading is liturgical song. It's so precious to be able to use the psalms and canticles of Scripture in our worship today. But how often do we actually sing them – and, as we do so, let joy overflow through us to our God?

C O L L E C T

Almighty Father,
you have given your only Son to die for our sins
and to rise again for our justification:
grant us so to put away the leaven of malice and wickedness
that we may always serve you
in pureness of living and truth;
through the merits of your Son Jesus Christ our Lord,
who is alive and reigns with you,
in the unity of the Holy Spirit,
one God, now and for ever.

Psalms **8**, 20, 21 *or* **5**, 6, (8)
Exodus 15.22 – 16.10
Colossians 1.15-end

Exodus 15.22 – 16.10

How quickly we move from celebration and thanksgiving to frustration and complaining. God's people, saved from the destructive might of Pharaoh, now find themselves trekking across the desert, hungry, thirsty and exhausted. Why have they come here? Wasn't life easier back 'home' in Egypt (16.3)?

We want to share with the whole world the good news that God has raised Jesus Christ from the dead. Still, receiving this message is hardly a ticket for life-long contentment, for us or anyone else. Those whose life is now hidden in God with the crucified and risen Christ can no longer remain comfortably at home among the things on earth; they have embarked on a demanding journey that can only end when Christ is fully revealed (Colossians 3.1-4). There are bound to be times when the old way of living looks attractive in comparison.

Yet, on the way of faith, by God's grace, our needs and struggles become occasions of more grace. His people are thirsty, and he helps them find water; his people are hungry, and he provides them with food. As long as they keep moving forwards, they keep finding new gifts, new wonders day by day. And, as they look out towards the far horizon, God's glory appears (16.10). He is all around them, guiding them, sustaining them.

Risen Christ,
for whom no door is locked, no entrance barred:
open the doors of our hearts,
that we may seek the good of others
and walk the joyful road of sacrifice and peace,
to the praise of God the Father.

COLLECT

Psalms 16, **30** *or* **119.1-32**
Exodus 16.11-end
Colossians 2.1-15

Exodus 16.11-end

Why could God not just miraculously transport the Israelites from the Red Sea to the Jordan? Why must they make their way through the desert? Why can't God just give us *now* what we believe he wants to give us in the end?

The answer is simple: because we are not yet ready to receive it. In the Sinai Peninsula, a sweet, flaky substance is naturally produced by a species of plant lice; perhaps that is part of the background to this passage, with the miracle being the dependability of the supply. Israel has to learn how to accept daily bread from God's hand. If they greedily try to get more, there will be just enough. And if they run out of time and come home with little, there will be just enough too. If they try to hoard it so they can control the supply themselves, it rots away. Yet, on the sixth day, God gives them a double portion that can be preserved, so there can be Sabbath time.

God begins to prepare his people for journey's end by teaching them to keep time: beginning each day by recalling our utter dependence on him, creating a weekly rhythm in which one day is set aside to rest in his presence. Whose time are we keeping this week?

COLLECT

Almighty Father,
you have given your only Son to die for our sins
and to rise again for our justification:
grant us so to put away the leaven of malice and wickedness
that we may always serve you
in pureness of living and truth;
through the merits of your Son Jesus Christ our Lord,
who is alive and reigns with you,
in the unity of the Holy Spirit,
one God, now and for ever.

Psalms **28**, 29 or 14, **15**, 16
Exodus 17
Colossians 2.16 – 3.11

Thursday 15 April

Exodus 17

In the wilderness, God has been testing his people (Exodus 15.25, 16.4). This is a difficult but critical theme in Scripture: Abraham leading Isaac up the mountain, Job's cries from the depths. Those whom he loves, God tests – and somehow they are blessed through it.

In this chapter, a line is crossed. No longer just 'complaining', the people are 'quarrelling'. And, in their quarrelling, *they* are testing *God*. The two names of the place spell this out: Massah and Meribah, 'Test' and 'Quarrel' (17.7). To start testing God is to fail in God's testing of us: 'Do not put the Lord your God to the test, as you tested him at Massah' (Deuteronomy 6.16) – a verse Jesus quotes when the devil suggests he launch himself from the pinnacle of the temple. As soon as we inch towards trying to force God's hand, to manipulate and control him, we have ceased to trust. We deny that he is our Maker and we are the people of his pasture (Psalm 95.6-9).

It is easy to lapse into quarrelling – at home, at work, at church – and easy to feel sure that, like the Israelites with Moses, we are only the unfortunate victims of other people's failures. Is it possible that, down this accommodating slope, we too might cross some dangerous lines?

Risen Christ,
for whom no door is locked, no entrance barred:
open the doors of our hearts,
that we may seek the good of others
and walk the joyful road of sacrifice and peace,
to the praise of God the Father.

COLLECT

Friday 16 April

Exodus 18.1-12

After murderous quarrelling and miraculous provision, and just before the climactic self-revelation of God on Sinai, the family shows up – the father-in-law Moses met on the run from Egypt, the wife he married before 'I am' sent him back there to God's people.

Moses might be excused for sighing deeply and trying to get through this unexpected visit as quickly as possible. Instead, he greets them warmly and is delighted to tell of everything God has been doing, focusing, as he did in the song of chapter 15, on how the Lord had delivered them. Jethro, priest of Midian, is thrilled to hear Moses' story and responds by blessing the God of Israel. Together, they share worship and food in God's presence.

However involved we are in the work of the gospel, our lives remain bound up, in countless ways, with that which has not yet recognized or fully embraced it. That is true of the depths of our own hearts, of the culture within whose currents we are bound to move, and of the human relationships that indelibly mark our story and identity. What is our response when, out of the blue, they come calling? Do we welcome them and share God's story with them, or are we too preoccupied with what we take to be God's urgent business?

COLLECT

Almighty Father,
you have given your only Son to die for our sins
and to rise again for our justification:
grant us so to put away the leaven of malice and wickedness
that we may always serve you
in pureness of living and truth;
through the merits of your Son Jesus Christ our Lord,
who is alive and reigns with you,
in the unity of the Holy Spirit,
one God, now and for ever.

Psalms 63, **84** or 20, 21, **23**
Exodus 18.13-end
Colossians 4.2-end

Exodus 18.13-end

The outsider sees things that the person immersed in the situation does not. It's the premise of many folk-tales and the rationale for spending money on consultants. Sometimes, though, the outsider is nearer than we think.

The morning after their celebration, Moses gets back to work; Jethro has some free time to watch. And what he sees is not good – 'You will surely wear yourself out, both you and these people with you.' Moses is isolated and overworked, and the people have to queue all day to get a response from him. Jethro spots the danger in Moses' acute sense of responsibility for God's people and makes recommendations about delegating, organizing and prioritizing. Moses adopts them in their entirety, Jethro leaves, and the Israelites are ready for the next stage of the journey.

Simple enough. But just think how Moses might have reacted. God has revealed his name to him, humiliated the regional superpower through him and guided him to provide food and drink for thousands of people in the treacherous desert. So, if Moses needs to hear something, won't God just tell him? Why should he take advice from a priest of Midian about how to make known to God's chosen people 'the statutes and instructions of God'?

Wisdom comes in many ways, but always as God's gift.

Risen Christ,
for whom no door is locked, no entrance barred:
open the doors of our hearts,
that we may seek the good of others
and walk the joyful road of sacrifice and peace,
to the praise of God the Father.

COLLECT

Easter Season

Monday 19 April

Luke 1.1-25

Luke writes to give Theophilus confidence (one of the meanings of the Greek word _asphaleian_ in verse 4) in the gospel, the good news of Jesus crucified and risen. To do this, he has had to spend time 'investigating everything carefully from the very first'. And this means going back to the beginning, in order to 'set down an orderly account of the events that have been fulfilled among us'.

So, he starts with Jesus' birth. But, to do that, he has to push further back, to the birth of John. And, because these first events are already the fulfilment of earlier promises, earlier events, Luke needs to write about them in a way that shows they have roots going back over centuries: to Elijah, to miraculous overcoming of childlessness in the cases of Samuel and Samson, to instructions in the desert about Nazarites and their vows.

It is not easy to keep a story about divine fulfilment 'orderly': there is something prodigal about the way God sows the word of promise and then nourishes it towards flowering and fruitfulness. Yet, all that abundant life meets in one life, one body, broken for all, raised in glory. In hearing again the story of this life from the beginning, our confidence in the gospel of life can grow stronger, deeper.

COLLECT

Almighty Father,
who in your great mercy gladdened the disciples
    with the sight of the risen Lord:
give us such knowledge of his presence with us,
that we may be strengthened and sustained by his risen life
and serve you continually in righteousness and truth;
through Jesus Christ your Son our Lord,
who is alive and reigns with you,
in the unity of the Holy Spirit,
one God, now and for ever.

Psalms **98**, 99, 100 *or* 32, **36**
Exodus 20.1-21
Luke 1.26-38

Luke 1.26-38

Six months after appearing to Zechariah in the temple, Gabriel speaks to Mary. It is one of the most famous scenes in Christian art. Yet Luke does no scene-setting for us at all. Where was she – at home or out and about? What was she doing – sitting down in tranquillity or busy with domestic chores? Through meditation as well as visual art, Christians have sought to fill in the background.

By contrast, the appearance of Gabriel to Zechariah was carefully set in place and time: at the right side of the altar of incense, at the time of the incense-offering. While Luke's narrative derives its rhythm from the movement between different locations (Jerusalem, Galilee, Judea, wilderness), his Gospel begins and ends in the temple. So, is that the central location? In one way, yes. Yet, at another level, it is radically displaced.

And this is the site of the displacement: in a distant town, a young woman receives God's word of favour and conceives in her womb God's Son, the eternal Word making his home among us, the place where God's glory is seen. It is not any location that makes this possible, but the exchange of invitation and acceptance: 'Here am I.' If we care to imagine the scene, may it be to help us share in the exchange.

Risen Christ,
you filled your disciples with boldness and fresh hope:
strengthen us to proclaim your risen life
and fill us with your peace,
to the glory of God the Father.

COLLECT

Wednesday 21 April

Luke 1.39-56

How many people will you greet today, and how many will greet you? It sounds a little old-fashioned. In our self-consciously informal culture, acknowledging the beginning of an encounter does not seem to demand much attention.

Addressed by Gabriel, Mary had wondered 'what sort of greeting this might be'. It became a greeting that changed her life, and the life of the world. Now, after a long journey, she greets Elizabeth, and this greeting too becomes transformative. The prophet whom Elizabeth is carrying in her womb kicks out for joy, and the Holy Spirit fills her so that she can cry out the prophetic word. That word in turn elicits from Mary the first of the three great prophetic songs in these chapters, each of which has found a home in the daily cycle of Christian prayer. Every evening, this meeting is remembered in our worship.

Meeting with another human being begins with greeting – warm or cold, formal or familiar. In that moment, dare we ask what the other might be carrying that could be a gift for us, or what we might be carrying that could be a gift for them? If something stirs within us, will we have time to wonder what it may be, and whether it also signals a movement of the Holy Spirit?

COLLECT

Almighty Father,
who in your great mercy gladdened the disciples
    with the sight of the risen Lord:
give us such knowledge of his presence with us,
that we may be strengthened and sustained by his risen life
and serve you continually in righteousness and truth;
through Jesus Christ your Son our Lord,
who is alive and reigns with you,
in the unity of the Holy Spirit,
one God, now and for ever.

Psalms **136** *or* **37***
Exodus 25.1-22
Luke 1.57-end

Thursday 22 April

Luke 1.57-end

It's easy to tease someone who has lost their voice for a day or two, as they despairingly mouth words and emit hoarse half-sounds. We may also know people whose lack of speech is a permanent condition – not a laughing matter. What would it be like to be speechless for nine months and then suddenly find your voice again?

Because he struggles to receive good news, Zechariah is overcome with inarticulacy. There should be great joy to share with Elizabeth, yet he cannot respond to her happiness in words. Others occasionally 'motion' to this isolated figure so that his wishes can be taken into account. The child is born, and, eventually, he is able to get a writing tablet and confirm the name: John. The struggle is over as he finally affirms the message he originally heard. At once, speech returns.

What does Zechariah do with this restored power? He praises God and prophesies. He sings a song of God's mercy: mercy stretching back through the generations, through prophets and forebears to Abraham, ancestor of all God's people; mercy that frees us to serve God without fear of darkness and death; tender mercy that means light and salvation here and now.

Only when we stop resisting the gift, and rest instead in God's mercy, will we find our real voice.

Risen Christ,
you filled your disciples with boldness and fresh hope:
strengthen us to proclaim your risen life
and fill us with your peace,
to the glory of God the Father.

COLLECT

Friday 23 April

George, martyr, patron of England

Ephesians 6.10-20

'Just as the first humans could fall from sonship of God into estrangement from Him, so do we all stand on the edge of the blade between night and the fullness of divine life. Sooner or later we are made to actually feel that this is the case.'

Edith Stein wrote those words well before she was taken to Auschwitz and murdered by the Nazis. Like George, soldier and martyr, she understood that to abide in God's life and not slip suddenly into night is no easy matter. Night will always seek ways to draw and drag us to itself.

The letter to the Ephesians begins with an outpouring of praise to God for all he has given us though Jesus Christ: adoption, redemption, forgiveness, the seal of the Spirit, the riches of his inheritance, a seat in the heavenly places, access to the Father. Yet here, just before its conclusion, we are told that we are enmeshed in a struggle – and, moreover, a struggle in which we are called to be not victorious heroes but faithful infantry soldiers who just manage to hold their ground, and who do not confuse their fights against other people or aspects of themselves with the one battle that really matters. Sooner or later, Stein says, we will realize how much.

COLLECT

God of hosts,
who so kindled the flame of love
in the heart of your servant George
that he bore witness to the risen Lord
by his life and by his death:
give us the same faith and power of love
that we who rejoice in his triumphs
may come to share with him the fullness of the resurrection;
through Jesus Christ your Son our Lord,
who is alive and reigns with you,
in the unity of the Holy Spirit,
one God, now and for ever.

Psalms 108, **110**, 111 *or* 41, **42**, 43
Exodus 29.1-9
Luke 2.21-40

Luke 2.21-40

'A sword will pierce your own soul too.' Traditionally, these words have been taken as prophecy of the pain of Jesus' mother in witnessing his execution. Some commentators, however, link them instead to the rest of Simeon's words to Mary, about the division that this child will cause within Israel (in the Greek, they come at the start of verse 35, not at the end as in the NRSV). She will feel within herself the distress of the conflicting responses to her son's ministry: a sign that will be opposed.

One line of interpretation is that, in these first two chapters of Luke, Mary represents Israel as a whole. She receives God's word to dwell within her. She celebrates that God has done great things for her, his servant. She brings into the world the one anointed by God to call the nations to know him. These are the acts of Israel. And Mary will also bear the confusion and opposition that this Messiah will evoke within Israel.

The new thing that began with Gabriel's greeting of Mary in Galilee comes for the first time to the centre of Israel's continuing life, the temple in Jerusalem. And, in the midst of the light of recognition, a shadow of darker anticipation is glimpsed. Does it also stretch out to us?

Almighty Father,
who in your great mercy gladdened the disciples
with the sight of the risen Lord:
give us such knowledge of his presence with us,
that we may be strengthened and sustained by his risen life
and serve you continually in righteousness and truth;
through Jesus Christ your Son our Lord,
who is alive and reigns with you,
in the unity of the Holy Spirit,
one God, now and for ever.

COLLECT

Monday 26 April

Mark the Evangelist

Psalms 37.23-end, 148
Isaiah 62.6-10 or
Ecclesiasticus 51.13-end
Acts 12.25 – 13.13

Acts 12.25 – 13.13

Poor Mark. This is his day, and yet all he gets to do in this passage is assist Barnabas and Paul (who is called 'Saul' here, as he is throughout his life when ministering in primarily Jewish contexts). It's not exactly a glamorous role in today's story of the enemy of the Gospel being temporarily blinded.

It is ironic that blindness is the curse that Paul calls down upon his opponent. Paul saw the good news of God in Christ as bad news that must be stamped out, until he met the risen Jesus and was struck blind. Assisted by Ananias and others, Paul came to see Jesus' work as good news, and Paul served that good news of Christ's reign all the way to the very centre of the Roman Empire. Ananias doesn't get much attention in Acts either, but his assisting Paul at a crucial point makes possible much of the amazing work Acts describes.

Perhaps Mark assisted the blind magician to come to see God's love as well as God's power. We don't know how Mark assisted the Jerusalem Christians during their crisis of famine and the crucial debate in Acts 15 about the validity of Paul's ministry amongst Gentiles. We just know he was there. Blessed Mark – faithful, present and mostly unsung as he helps or is rejected – an icon of of the precious spiritual gift of being there.

COLLECT

Almighty God,
who enlightened your holy Church
through the inspired witness of your evangelist Saint Mark:
grant that we, being firmly grounded in the truth of the gospel,
may be faithful to its teaching both in word and deed;
through Jesus Christ your Son our Lord,
who is alive and reigns with you,
in the unity of the Holy Spirit,
one God, now and for ever.

Psalms **139** *or* **48**, 52
Exodus 32.15-34
Luke 3.1-14

Luke 3.1-14

What Mark introduces more simply as 'the beginning of the good news of Jesus Christ', namely, the message of John the Baptist, Luke places specifically in relation to a number of powers: Tiberius, Pontius Pilate, Herod, Philip, Lysanius and Caiaphas. These are people who, in one context or another, would have been called 'Lord'. But John proclaims another Lord, whose way he intends to prepare, and who has power and authority to level every field and save all that lives.

Language of Jesus as 'Lord' is not unproblematic, and most especially after centuries of colonizers and slavers both proclaiming Jesus as 'master' (the Greek *kyrios* can be translated as that also) and forcing other people made in God's image to use that title when addressing them. That's actually why I want to reclaim the language that 'Jesus is Lord'. There are always mere human beings and harmful powers wanting to claim that title: rulers of nations, bosses in a workplace, abusive people, or powers of greed, the need to achieve, an inner voice that says 'you're not worth anything' or 'I must control everything'. So many would-be powers and principalities. When I say that 'Jesus is Lord', I mean to tell all of them that they can go away – that position has been filled. However odd it may seem, claiming that power for Jesus has been for me a route to empowerment in the Spirit with which Jesus baptizes.

Almighty God,
whose Son Jesus Christ is the resurrection and the life:
raise us, who trust in him,
from the death of sin to the life of righteousness,
that we may seek those things which are above,
where he reigns with you
in the unity of the Holy Spirit,
one God, now and for ever.

COLLECT

Wednesday 28 April

Psalms 135 *or* 119.57-80
Exodus 33
Luke 3.15-22

Luke 3.15-22

John the Baptist preached fire, though he didn't think he was bringing the flames. He proclaimed that 'One is coming who is more powerful than I', one who would have a winnowing shovel in hand and would bring the fire as well as the Holy Spirit. If you did a double-take at the word 'shovel', you're an observant reader, as most English translations say it's a fork instead – but that translation is misguided, as scholar Robert L. Webb argues, and it does make a difference. Winnowing involves three stages: separating expendable chaff from useful wheat, disposing of the chaff, and storing the wheat. The first stage is done with a fork, and the second and third with a shovel. John hoped that Jesus would be the man with the shovel, and John was looking forward to the fireworks that would consume the wicked, as well as to the Spirit who would save the grain. We see in Luke 7 that John was sorely disappointed in half of that hope.

Jesus does not come to burn the wicked to a cinder. He spends his childhood almost entirely in an obscure village in Galilee. He teaches, heals, and suffers; he consorts with 'sinners'; he is executed by a Roman governor for treason and is raised by God. He baptizes with the Holy Spirit, but not with fire. 'Blessed are the merciful', and Jesus' blessing upon those who don't stumble over him, say nearly the same thing.

COLLECT

Almighty God,
whose Son Jesus Christ is the resurrection and the life:
raise us, who trust in him,
from the death of sin to the life of righteousness,
that we may seek those things which are above,
where he reigns with you
in the unity of the Holy Spirit,
one God, now and for ever.

Psalms **118** *or* 56, **57**, (63*)
Exodus 34.1-10,27-end
Luke 4.1-13

Luke 4.1-13

When Shakespeare said in *The Merchant of Venice* that the devil can quote Scripture, I'm confident he had Jesus' temptation in mind. An accusing power shows up quoting the Bible to justify one human being exercising power over others and over creation that belongs rightly to God – a situation all too familiar to any student of human history, and indeed to any participant in the networks of human relationships that form cultures, societies and economies, as well as smaller but equally intricate webs.

Jesus quotes Scripture right back. That in itself doesn't necessarily say much; duelling over power with quotations from Scripture can become what I call 'biblical whack-a-mole', after the carnival game. Person A quotes verse 1; Person B whacks it with verse 2. Person A quotes verse 3; Person B whacks it with verse 4. The process repeats, tempers rise, and the speed of biblical 'whacking' increases. But, when it's all over, everyone involved still knows that nothing has been resolved; it will all erupt again as soon as the next person drops a coin into the machine. And the world just yawns, if it notices at all – there are far more serious, more important and even more amusing things going on elsewhere.

What says not only that Jesus wins, but also what that victory means for us, is not how many verses Jesus can quote, but how Jesus' manner of life provides us with an interpretive lens.

Risen Christ,
faithful shepherd of your Father's sheep:
teach us to hear your voice
and to follow your command,
that all your people may be gathered into one flock,
to the glory of God the Father.

COLLECT

Friday 30 April

Psalms **33** *or* **51**, 54
Exodus 35.20 – 36.7
Luke 4.14-30

Luke 4.14-30

These days, it seems everyone is into mission statements. In this passage, Jesus offers his own, using language from Isaiah. It's not a single quotation, but a kind of DJ-style 'mash-up' between two passages. When Jesus steps to the front of the synagogue, he reads from Isaiah 61. But, at one point, Jesus jumps off to Isaiah 42. Odds are that this would have been on an entirely different scroll, leaving Jesus in front of both, like a DJ in front of dual turntables or iPods.

What an odd sight that would make! So, what gets Jesus 'mashing it up'? It's when he reaches a phrase from Isaiah 61.2, namely 'the day of vengeance of our God'. That's when he cross-fades (no pun intended) to the other scroll, substituting Isaiah 42.7's phrase, 'the recovery of sight to the blind'. He cuts out the vengeance and substitutes healing. That's what Jesus considers righteous – that is, the right relationship he has with humanity and that we ought to have with one another.

That's something worth remembering when I feel truly wronged and I want to respond in kind. If the only person who gets the title of 'Lord' refuses to lord it over others, how can I think of myself as judge or jury, let alone executioner, with respect to someone else?

COLLECT

Almighty God,
whose Son Jesus Christ is the resurrection and the life:
raise us, who trust in him,
from the death of sin to the life of righteousness,
that we may seek those things which are above,
where he reigns with you
in the unity of the Holy Spirit,
one God, now and for ever.

Psalms 139, 146
Proverbs 4.10-18
James 1.1-12

Philip and James, Apostles

Proverbs 4.10-18

One of my many paid avocations supporting my mostly unpaid vocation as a teacher in and facilitator of Christian community has been work as a teacher of self-defence, including techniques based on *aikido*, in which an attacker's force is the weapon against the attacker. Sometimes I think God might be a practitioner of *aikido*.

What I mean is illustrated vividly in this passage from Proverbs. If my morning commute brings me near someone who tries to race ahead at the side of the road and then cut into my lane of traffic, I can respond by driving as though it were up to me to see that such wickedness is not rewarded, driving as close as I can to the bumper of the car ahead of me and trying to cut the interloper off instead. I have found this to be a highly efficient course of action – that is, if my goal is to raise my blood pressure.

If I'm trying to get to work on time and in one piece, though, I'm better off keeping my eyes on that particular prize. If Proverbs is right, unrighteousness is its own punishment, and God doesn't need me to punish. As a limited human being, I'm healthiest and happiest when I let God play the role of God – and so mercy is also its own reward.

COLLECT

Almighty Father,
whom truly to know is eternal life:
teach us to know your Son Jesus Christ
as the way, the truth, and the life;
that we may follow the steps
of your holy apostles Philip and James,
and walk steadfastly in the way that leads to your glory;
through Jesus Christ your Son our Lord,
who is alive and reigns with you,
in the unity of the Holy Spirit,
one God, now and for ever.

Monday 3 May

Psalms **145** *or* **71**
Numbers 9.15-end, 10.33-end
Luke 4.38-end

Luke 4.38-end

Here we see demons display their power: they have acquired knowledge of Jesus' identity as God's anointed Son, and they use that knowledge, the knowledge of Jesus' true or secret name, to try in effect to exorcise Jesus, to control him. Were demonic power sufficient to overcome the power of God's love, the result would be isolation in brokenness – God's son torn from God's people, division overcoming reconciliation. That's what demonic power tries to do, after all: get knowledge to wield power over others, and use power over others to isolate them from one another as well as from God.

But Jesus' power calls all people – far off and nearby – to healing and reconciliation in loving service. Jesus restores all who come to him to wholeness in relationships as well as in bodies; he cures conditions perceived as causing impurity and posing danger to the community. Our teacher here is the mother-in-law of Simon Peter. Jesus uses the same power of naming to rebuke the fever – and God's love heals, bringing her from a bed out of sight into full membership and service among disciples. In the next passage, Jesus uses the power of naming and truth-telling to bring a similar call to Peter. And some day, in God's story of truth and reconciliation, we will see that power in such fullness that none of God's servants, female or male, will be cast out of sight in anonymity again.

COLLECT

Almighty God,
who through your only-begotten Son Jesus Christ
have overcome death and opened to us the gate of
    everlasting life:
grant that, as by your grace going before us
    you put into our minds good desires,
so by your continual help
we may bring them to good effect;
through Jesus Christ our risen Lord,
who is alive and reigns with you,
in the unity of the Holy Spirit,
one God, now and for ever.

Psalms **19**, 147.1-12 *or* **73**
Numbers 11.1-33
Luke 5.1-11

Luke 5.1-11

Jesus here calls his first disciples while they are fishing – something modern readers might have experienced as a relaxing opportunity to catch sun and quiet – and perhaps a fish or two. Fishing wasn't at all like that for Peter, however. The life of a first-century fisher was one of constant anxiety, asking day after day: 'How can I catch enough fish for my family to survive?' After renting or buying the boat, after paying Rome's hefty taxes, after mending the nets, with the right winds and currents, and considerable luck, will there be enough fish?

Jesus calls amid their worry, and they catch a miraculous abundance of fish – so many, in fact, that the catch threatens to break the nets and even to swamp the boats, potentially ending life as well as livelihood. In that moment, the most fundamental and urgent question in the fishers' lives changes from 'How can I catch enough fish to survive?' to 'How can I gather enough people to take in this abundance?' They become fishers of people.

Are you anxious? Is it hard to think about setting aside the nets to go where Jesus calls? Perhaps the first step towards a life of abundant joy and peace is to intentionally shift that basic question from 'How can I get enough to survive?' to 'How can I gather enough neighbours to enjoy God's abundance?'

> Risen Christ,
> your wounds declare your love for the world
> and the wonder of your risen life:
> give us compassion and courage
> to risk ourselves for those we serve,
> to the glory of God the Father.

COLLECT

Wednesday 5 May

Psalms **30**, 147.13-end *or* **77**
Numbers 12
Luke 5.12-26

Luke 5.12-26

Our Christ has been and remains such a bother – especially to those who want to withdraw from 'sinners' in his name. The Jesus of the Gospels, for whom we claim the title of God's anointed, simply refuses to do it.

This is not to say, of course, that Jesus is willing to stand idly by when he's got a sinner in front of him. Not according to the canonical Gospels, at least. Instead, he takes the initiative in pronouncing God's forgiveness and showering the sinner with God's gifts. He doesn't wait for contrition, confession or amendment of life before showing mercy, as is obvious when he pronounces forgiveness for the paralysed man. If only he'd stopped there, we religious people might yet be able to get away with using his name as a symbol of respectable and tame – but naive and irrelevant – piety.

He doesn't stop, though. Jesus goes on to claim – most shockingly of all – that the authority with and example by which he does this is God's. Jesus' 'golden rule' isn't 'refrain from doing to others what you wouldn't want done to you', but '*do* to others what you'd want them to do with you'. And so, those of us who claim to follow him can't stand idly by when confronted by a sinner: we will be too busy rushing to invite and embrace, in God's name.

COLLECT

Almighty God,
who through your only-begotten Son Jesus Christ
have overcome death and opened to us the gate of
    everlasting life:
grant that, as by your grace going before us
    you put into our minds good desires,
so by your continual help
we may bring them to good effect;
through Jesus Christ our risen Lord,
who is alive and reigns with you,
in the unity of the Holy Spirit,
one God, now and for ever.

Psalms **57**, 148 or **78.1-39***
Numbers 13.1-3,17-end
Luke 5.27-end

Luke 5.27-end

Jesus' manner of life becomes a source of controversy, scandal, and strife even before his death. One reason is that, as his friends and enemies agree, he insists on indulging – repeatedly and not at all discreetly – in intimate fellowship and breaking bread with people seen as 'sinners' by those whom society called 'good'. He furthermore claims, as we saw in the story of his healing the paralysed, that God does and orders the same. He doesn't let this go without explanation. Jesus here uses two sets of metaphors to describe what he is doing in God's name. He – and therefore God, if we take seriously Jesus' claim that he acts with God's authority and Christianity's claims about incarnation – is a physician. He – and therefore God, according to creedal Christianity – is a bridegroom. Both roles are meaningless without relationship and intimate contact.

This idea about God's character is about as far from the Platonic 'unmoved mover' or the impersonal 'Force' from *Star Wars* films as one can get. If a man is without his beloved, no costume, cake or setting can make him a groom any more than his beloved could entirely on her own become a bride. A 'doctor', if she never has contact with patients, is simply an unemployed person with an extra piece of paper. And, if we are indeed made in God's image, we too are defined by our relationships. The faithfulness with which we follow Jesus correlates directly and positively with the eagerness with which we break bread with 'sinners'.

Risen Christ,
your wounds declare your love for the world
and the wonder of your risen life:
give us compassion and courage
to risk ourselves for those we serve,
to the glory of God the Father.

COLLECT

Luke 6.1-11

I have a great deal of sympathy for Jonah, who struggled and became whale vomit, and finally gave in to God's call to preach fire and brimstone, only to have the Ninevites repent and be forgiven and blessed. I admit it: It's very satisfying to *know* that I'm right. It's even more satisfying when I *know* that others are wrong. And it's all too tempting to get out my snorkel for a good dive into self-righteous self-pity when I have opportunity to feel that I'm *persecuted* because I am right and they are wrong.

So, I'm also sympathetic towards the small group of scribes and Pharisees looking to trip up Jesus on the sabbath. And let's be as clear as Scripture is that Pharisees are not a monolithic bunch of villains. Paul identifies as one throughout his life (Acts 23.10, Philippian 3.5), and others are participants in apostolic council (Acts 15.5) and icons of prayerful tolerance (Acts 5.34). Using 'Pharisee' as a synonym for 'hypocrite' is rightly received by many Jews as a symptom of antisemitism – an insult to the Jew we call Christ as well as to his God, who gave the Torah.

So, I'll imitate Pharisees like Gamaliel. In daily life, my most frequent actions become the easiest and most habitual. Do I want to become a person habitually looking for faults, or a person habitually finding healing? Only one of those habits brings lasting joy.

COLLECT

Almighty God,
who through your only-begotten Son Jesus Christ
have overcome death and opened to us the gate of
    everlasting life:
grant that, as by your grace going before us
    you put into our minds good desires,
so by your continual help
we may bring them to good effect;
through Jesus Christ our risen Lord,
who is alive and reigns with you,
in the unity of the Holy Spirit,
one God, now and for ever.

Psalms **146**, 150 *or* **76**, 79
Numbers 14.26-end
Luke 6.12-26

Luke 6.12-26

The Beatitudes are so familiar to churchgoing types that it's easy to get caught up in their poetry and forget that they were addressed to real people in their actual situation. Those who dropped what their culture said any decent person would do – namely to stay for life in the village with the extended family to care for the young and the ageing and to work for the family's survival and honour – to roam after some teacher, healer and agitator risked becoming the sort of person Jesus calls 'blessed'. Destitute. Hungry. Grieving. Reviled and outcast utterly. We forget how shocking it is to contemplate that a decision to leave career, home, spouse, siblings, parents and children could be decent, let alone blessed by God. Think of how often an abused spouse or child is told by churchgoing types to tough it out for Jesus rather than to leave for God's sake. But the latter action is one Jesus praised (Luke 18.28-30).

Such a costly course! How on earth could that be Good News? Wouldn't it be better to be among the comfortable and respectable folks at home upon whom Jesus cried woe? Not if those called away from conventional respectability and therefore family and society form an unconventional family in which all care for all – and which even relatives who had done the casting out would be welcome to join.

Risen Christ,
your wounds declare your love for the world
and the wonder of your risen life:
give us compassion and courage
to risk ourselves for those we serve,
to the glory of God the Father.

Luke 6.27-38

The golden rule, 'Do to others as you would have them do to you' (v.31), is a central tenet of many religions and ethical systems. We should treat each other in a decent manner, no less than the manner in which we would like to be treated. It is a short step from here to basic declarations of human rights: we have a right to just treatment and a responsibility to ensure justice for others. In fact, this ethic of reciprocity underpins our modern concept of human rights. But Jesus shows us that the context and impetus for the rule is not a system of reciprocal rights – 'I'll treat you well so that you'll treat me well' – but the astonishing, overwhelming generosity we have already received from God.

'A good measure, pressed down, shaken together, running over' (v.38): this is how we are to understand the munificence of God. He gives to excess rather than doling out carefully measured portions. Never mind what is fair; his love is simply poured out unstintingly. It is because God is like this that we too can afford to be generous in our loving and giving and doing good. It is simply another way of letting the goodness of God poured into *our* lives spill out into *others*'. For whom would we hesitate to pour such a generous measure today?

COLLECT

God our redeemer,
you have delivered us from the power of darkness
and brought us into the kingdom of your Son:
grant, that as by his death he has recalled us to life,
so by his continual presence in us he may raise us
     to eternal joy;
through Jesus Christ your Son our Lord,
who is alive and reigns with you,
in the unity of the Holy Spirit,
one God, now and for ever.

Luke 6.39-end

Jesus continues his ethical teaching apace with illustrations from contemporary life. Ditches, specks and logs, figs and brambles are all put to use to berate hypocrisy and make clear the link between actions and the attitude of the heart. Finally, the crux of the matter: 'Why do you call me "Lord, Lord", and not do what I tell you?' Words are all very well, but it is *actions* that count, and so the warning comes. If you listen and nod but fail to act, you will be like the foolish man who built his house upon the sand. The edifice may go up quickly and look impressive, but it will not be up for long when the floods come.

Jesus knew all about building houses – he was a carpenter. He knew that the digging of deep foundations is a back-breaking job, requiring time, effort and commitment.

It is messy digging down to clear the site, removing large stones and rubbish, to ensure a flat surface on which to build. Similarly, there are no short cuts when it comes to putting down the foundations of faith. It is difficult to clear away those things in our lives that impede spiritual growth, but we are helped in this work by the one who is himself the precious cornerstone, Jesus Christ.

Risen Christ,
by the lakeside you renewed your call to your disciples:
help your Church to obey your command
and draw the nations to the fire of your love,
to the glory of God the Father.

COLLECT

75

Wednesday 12 May

Luke 7.1-10

Words without deeds may be worthless, as we learned in yesterday's reading – but, for Jesus, such is his integrity that word and deed are inseparable. How could they be when he is, literally, the Word made flesh?

In antiquity, miraculous healings were thought to be possible only via direct contact with the sick. It is remarkable, then, that the centurion believes in the power of Jesus to heal without requiring physical proximity. Indeed, Luther understood this passage to contain a double miracle: the first miracle is the centurion's faith, the second is the healing word of Christ.

'Only speak the word, and let my servant be healed.' We do not know which word Jesus uttered to heal the sick servant. But we do recognize this phrase as one we say for ourselves at the Eucharist: 'Lord, I am not worthy to receive you, but only say the word and I shall be healed.' We each know what that word would be for us and, like the centurion, we, too, reach towards the miracle of faith that trusts entirely in the Word made flesh and his ability to restore us to wholeness.

COLLECT

God our redeemer,
you have delivered us from the power of darkness
and brought us into the kingdom of your Son:
grant, that as by his death he has recalled us to life,
so by his continual presence in us he may raise us
    to eternal joy;
through Jesus Christ your Son our Lord,
who is alive and reigns with you,
in the unity of the Holy Spirit,
one God, now and for ever.

Psalms 110, 150
Isaiah 52.7-end
Hebrews 7.[11-25] 26-end

Hebrews 7.[11-25] 26-end

'God is gone up with a merry noise: and the Lord with the sound of the trump!'

At the college in which I work, we celebrate Ascension Day with a service of Choral Matins from the tower at 8am. Come rain or shine, the choir and up to 60 students clamber up a narrow staircase and out onto the roof for this annual ritual. There is a desire on this of all days to be *high up*, a little closer to the heavens into which Jesus has gone.

Hebrews makes clear that Jesus ascends as our great high priest. Christ, as high priest, reconciled the human race to God in his body, offering his own blood as the supreme sacrifice for sin. As he ascends into heaven, he takes us with him, our human nature transformed and glorified by his saving love.

Nevertheless, for the moment we remain earthbound creatures who will have to traipse back down the tower for breakfast after Matins. There is, though, a sense in which we have been drawn into the worship of the heavenly host for a brief moment, catching a glimpse of the Lord in glory sitting down at the right hand of the Majesty on high (Hebrews 1.3). It is this glimpse that we carry with us to inspire and encourage and to share with those around us.

> Grant, we pray, almighty God,
> that as we believe your only-begotten Son
> our Lord Jesus Christ
> to have ascended into the heavens,
> so we in heart and mind may also ascend
> and with him continually dwell;
> who is alive and reigns with you,
> in the unity of the Holy Spirit,
> one God, now and for ever.

COLLECT

Friday 14 May

Matthias the Apostle

Psalms 16, 147.1-12
1 Samuel 2.27-35
Acts 2.37-end

Acts 2.37-end

Today, we commemorate Matthias the Apostle, who filled the place of Judas, the betrayer. Little is known of Matthias, other than that he was a member of the group that had followed Jesus throughout his ministry – from the baptism of John until the Ascension (Acts 2.22). It is perhaps fanciful to wonder whether, having replaced Judas in the Twelve, Matthias reflected much on the actions of the betrayer; who would want Judas as a predecessor?

Of course, in a way, we all follow in Judas' steps. Despite our best intentions, we betray Christ through ignorance, weakness or our own deliberate fault. St Philip Neri (1515–95) uttered the following prayer: 'Lord, beware of this Philip or he will betray you! Lay your hand upon my head, for without you there is not a sin I may not commit this day.'

Let us ask God to keep his hand on us today and, if we fall, pray that we may have the grace to repent in earnest, as did those first Israelites, 'cut to the heart' when they heard how they had betrayed the promise of God in Christ (v.37).

COLLECT

Almighty God,
who in the place of the traitor Judas
chose your faithful servant Matthias
to be of the number of the Twelve:
preserve your Church from false apostles
and, by the ministry of faithful pastors and teachers,
keep us steadfast in your truth;
through Jesus Christ your Son our Lord,
who is alive and reigns with you,
in the unity of the Holy Spirit,
one God, now and for ever.

Psalms 21, **47** *or* 96, **97**, 100
Numbers 21.4-9
Luke 7.18-35

Luke 7.18-35

It's easy for our expectations to blind us. In fact, it's so easy that it even happens to John the Baptist: 'Are you the one who is to come, or are we to wait for another?' Having preached a stern message of judgement and repentance out in the wilderness, the grace-filled ministry of Jesus is not quite what he expected. But it is not John's misapprehension that Jesus is concerned about: wisdom will out (v.35), and John, when he hears how the prophecy of Isaiah is being fulfilled in Jesus, will have the wisdom and courage to see that Jesus exceeds his messianic expectations in a way that he could not have anticipated.

It is, instead, the misconceptions of 'this generation' that Jesus rails against. What are they *like*? They are certainly not the children of wisdom, but rather those who taunt and complain in an infantile manner that the behaviour of God's prophets is unsatisfactory, being either too ascetic or too libertine. It is reminiscent of the accusations often levelled by contemporary Christians against those whom they see as 'the others': too conservative, too liberal, too intellectual, too literalist. But wisdom will be vindicated by her children. Let us aspire to be among them.

Grant, we pray, almighty God,
that as we believe your only-begotten Son
our Lord Jesus Christ
to have ascended into the heavens,
so we in heart and mind may also ascend
and with him continually dwell;
who is alive and reigns with you,
in the unity of the Holy Spirit,
one God, now and for ever.

COLLECT

Monday 17 May

Luke 7.36-end

Yet again, Jesus eschews the social norms of his day. It is one–nil for the outcasts when Jesus, friend of tax-collectors and sinners, comes to dinner at the house of Simon the Pharisee. The story assures us beyond doubt that what counts for Jesus are the intentions of the heart.

In terms of hospitality, Simon's behaviour is lacking, but not rude. To provide water for guests to wash their feet is well attested, but it was not a normative practice; a kiss of greeting was accepted but not mandatory; anointing the feet was very unusual outside the family. Simon's manners are correct, but *merely* correct. The woman, on the other hand, has behaved in an outrageous manner, displaying a level of intimacy that is embarrassing the host within his own house. Her actions enable Simon to make a judgement about Jesus. This 'teacher' whom he invited to dinner has proved unworthy. It doesn't take a prophet to realize what kind of woman is touching Jesus: the loosing of the hair and kissing of the feet pretty much give it away! But, despite this, it is Simon who receives censure. Jesus sees the heart of both, and it is the love and gratitude of the penitent that is cherished, whatever form that takes.

COLLECT

O God the King of glory,
you have exalted your only Son Jesus Christ
with great triumph to your kingdom in heaven:
we beseech you, leave us not comfortless,
but send your Holy Spirit to strengthen us
and exalt us to the place where our Saviour Christ
    is gone before,
who is alive and reigns with you,
in the unity of the Holy Spirit,
one God, now and for ever.

Psalms 98, **99**, 100 *or* **106*** (or 103)
Numbers 22.36 – 23.12
Luke 8.1-15

Luke 8.1-15

Vincent van Gogh painted an evocative picture entitled *The Sower*. In it, a solitary figure walks along a field throwing enormous seeds towards the viewer; they almost seem to come out of the picture. It is an image that prompts us to ask not 'what kind of soil am I?', as the text would have, but rather 'what kind of sower?'

Imagine you are the one in charge of planting. You are sent out with a bag full of seeds to scatter – seeds packed full of life waiting to germinate: your gifts, hopes, deeds, energy and love. How generous will you be in dispersing this precious seed? How liberal in scattering love, forgiveness, time and talents, sometimes in places, or among people, who will yield little return?

Will you be extravagant, as the Divine Sower, who casts seed far and wide – on the paths and rocks as well as the good, safe soil? Or will you be really rather careful, even miserly? The seed we scatter will not always take root, but we must take this risk. Let us learn what God is like from this parable: Jesus' description of the Father is one of boundless love and mercy, scattering his grace abundantly, shamelessly indiscriminate among all people and situations. We are all called to be such sowers.

Risen, ascended Lord,
as we rejoice at your triumph,
fill your Church on earth with power and compassion,
that all who are estranged by sin
may find forgiveness and know your peace,
to the glory of God the Father.

COLLECT

81

Psalms 2, **29** *or* 110, **111**, 112
Numbers 23.13-end
Luke 8.16-25

Luke 8.16-25

Over the next three days, we will witness Jesus exhibiting his power in different realms. Today, as he calms the storm, it is over the natural order. Tomorrow, in the exorcism of the Gerasene demoniac, it will be over the spiritual order. The next day, we will see Jesus' power over the physical order when he cures the woman with the haemorrhage and, climactically, we witness his power over death as he raises Jairus' daughter from the dead. It is an intensive and all-encompassing teaching programme for the disciples!

The watchwords for each story are *fear* and *faith*. Today's episode is a basic lesson in anxiety management for the disciples. It's just them and Jesus, together in a boat sailing across the lake. A tranquil setting: what could possibly go wrong? But, all of a sudden, the wind changes and there is trouble at sea. Panic ensues, and the disciples, even while in the presence of Christ, the source of life, fear death. Whether or not we have faced a near-death situation, we know what it is to fear. It is debilitating, and faith can seem to evaporate. Perhaps it is worth reflecting on the response of the disciples to their plea. In the ensuing calm, they are still afraid, but now for a different reason. They fear not the power of the elements, but rather the power of Christ: a fear tinged with awe. This is the fear which will lead to love; the love which, when made perfect, casts out *all* fear (1 John 4.18).

COLLECT

O God the King of glory,
you have exalted your only Son Jesus Christ
with great triumph to your kingdom in heaven:
we beseech you, leave us not comfortless,
but send your Holy Spirit to strengthen us
and exalt us to the place where our Saviour Christ
    is gone before,
who is alive and reigns with you,
in the unity of the Holy Spirit,
one God, now and for ever.

Psalms **24**, 72 *or* 113, **115**
Numbers 24
Luke 8.26-39

Luke 8.26-39

Encountering serious mental or spiritual illness can be a frightening experience. Sufferers may behave in a way that is unexpected, uncontrollable and threatening. In this Gospel story, *everyone* is afraid: everyone, that is, except Jesus. The Gerasenes are afraid of the demoniac, keeping him chained up outside the city. The demoniac himself is afraid of torment on encountering Jesus – or, rather, that which possesses him is terrified by the power of the Son of the Most High God. The dramatic exorcism itself provokes a mixed response. In the man formerly known as 'Legion', fear has given way to faith, as he sits at the feet of Jesus. But, for the townsfolk, fear has multiplied – indeed, they are 'seized with a *great* fear'. A violent madman was just about manageable, but someone who wields such power in the spiritual realm is truly terrifying. In Jesus they perceive a man who really is *un*manageable – and they are right!

Fear as a response to God and his deeds is a well-attested aspect of biblical faith, from patriarch to psalmist to Paul. In the same way that the disciples feared the actions of Jesus in yesterday's reading, wondering 'Who is this?', so the Gerasenes fear him now. The only difference is in response. Instead of being drawn into faith, they allow fear to separate them from God. They forget that to fear God is to grow to know him, and that this fear is the beginning of wisdom (Proverbs 1.7)

> Risen, ascended Lord,
> as we rejoice at your triumph,
> fill your Church on earth with power and compassion,
> that all who are estranged by sin
> may find forgiveness and know your peace,
> to the glory of God the Father.

COLLECT

Friday 21 May

Psalms **28**, 30 *or* **139**
Numbers 27.12-end
Luke 8.40-end

Luke 8.40-end

Power, fear and faith come together once again in these two stories of healing. In a state of ritual impurity that would 'contaminate', the woman with the haemorrhage should not have been found in the midst of a large crowd – but desperate circumstances call for desperate measures. When forced to confess, she understandably comes forth with fear and trembling; not only has she 'taken' power from Jesus secretly, she has also made him unclean. Her exposure is essential: it is contact with Jesus that she needs, not simply anonymous access to his power. Her triumph of faith over fear may have been due to desperation, but it has opened her up to the working of God's power.

Jesus' words to Jairus present a similar challenge: 'Do not fear. Only believe, and she will be saved.' No pressure! To believe that, in Jesus, the defeat of death is possible requires a different order of faith: faith in the *impossible* rather than the simply *improbable*. But Jairus, like the haemorrhaging woman, is desperate. Theirs is not 'blind faith' of the sort that Richard Dawkins rails against – an ignorant belief without evidence. Rather, it is a deliberate choice to place absolute trust in Christ. In this faith, it is fear that dissolves, for we know that, whatever the outcome to our predicament, the love that defeats death will sustain us.

COLLECT

O God the King of glory,
you have exalted your only Son Jesus Christ
with great triumph to your kingdom in heaven:
we beseech you, leave us not comfortless,
but send your Holy Spirit to strengthen us
and exalt us to the place where our Saviour Christ
    is gone before,
who is alive and reigns with you,
in the unity of the Holy Spirit,
one God, now and for ever.

Psalms 42, **43** *or* 120, **121**, 122
Numbers 32.1-27
Luke 9.1-17

Saturday 22 May

Luke 9.1-17

'You give them something to eat.' Jesus' command to the disciples seems, on the surface, to set them up as stooges. Despite their concern for the crowd as the day grows dim, they are not exactly equipped for mass catering. Is this, then, a joke?

In Luke's version of events, the disciples respond by giving Jesus what they have and obeying his instruction to organize the people. It is Christ himself who provides the food – his abundance from their paucity – but the role of the disciples is essential in providing this hospitality. Jesus is the supreme delegator when it comes to meeting the needs of others. When we come before him with problems, the answer may often be: 'you do it'. This doesn't imply we have all the resources ourselves, but rather that we should attend to how we may participate in Christ's work. Sometimes it means giving him what we have, that it may be blessed and broken and distributed. And sometimes it means giving our very selves for that same purpose, remembering that what is placed in the hands of Christ, to be blessed and broken, is *transformed* by him and able to satisfy the needs of those for whom we are concerned.

'You give them something to eat.' A joke? Far from it. By their participation in the work of Christ, the disciples are indeed able to set food before the 5,000.

Risen, ascended Lord,
as we rejoice at your triumph,
fill your Church on earth with power and compassion,
that all who are estranged by sin
may find forgiveness and know your peace,
to the glory of God the Father.

COLLECT

A message to readers of
Reflections for Daily Prayer

This will be the last issue of *Reflections for Daily Prayer* in its current quarterly printed format.

It is hoped that the series may continue in another format in the future.

To ensure you are the first to hear about any future plans and any other new Church House Publishing products, please sign up for our e-newsletters at **www.chpublishing.co.uk/enewsletters**.

Common Worship: Daily Prayer

Daily Prayer is ideal for anyone
wanting to follow a regular pattern
of prayer, praise and Bible-reading.
The material may be used in small
groups or individually.

£22.50 (Hardback)
978 0 7151 2073 6
202 x 125mm, 896 pages

Time to Pray

Compact, soft-case volume offers a user-friendly
resource for praying through the week.
The simple, accessible structure
allows even those with little time
on their hands the opportunity to
'recharge' for a few minutes
each day. Includes Prayer During
the Day (for every single day of
the week), Night Prayer and
selected psalms from *Common
Worship: Daily Prayer*. To be used
by individuals or small groups.

£12.99 (Soft case)
978 0 7151 2122 7
199 x 125mm, 112 pages

Leading Common Worship Intercessions

A simple guide
Doug Chaplin

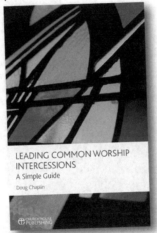

This is the essential guide for anyone – lay or ordained –
who leads intercessions in their local church. Doug
Chaplin's straightforward, 'how to' approach offers both a
source of inspiration for experienced intercessors and a
training tool for beginners. Includes sample forms of
prayer, important dos and don'ts, practical exercises and
checklists.

£5.99
ISBN 978 0 7151 4200 4
198 x 129mm, 80 pages